The Darling of My Heart

TWO THOUSAND YEARS OF IRISH LOVE WRITING

The Darling of My Heart

TWO THOUSAND YEARS OF IRISH LOVE WRITING

Compiled and edited by
Laurence Flanagan

Gill & Macmillan

Published in Ireland by
Gill & Macmillan Ltd
Goldenbridge
Dublin 8
with associated companies throughout the world

Design and print origination by Identikit Design Consultants, Dublin
Printed in Ireland by ColourBooks Ltd, Dublin

A catalogue record is available for this book
from the British Library.

1   3   5   4   2

For my father and mother
and my sisters, Kathleen and Maureen

Contents

Introduction

The compiling of a work such as this suffers from several constraints. There are a number of items that simply must be included. The great heroic romances of Ireland—the Deirdre story from the so-called Ulster Cycle and that of Diarmaid and Gráinne—are inevitable, as is at least one of the 'wooing' tales. For myself, 'For a Dead Wife' by Muiríoch Albanach Ó Dálaigh is an essential; for most people at least part of 'Cúirt an Mheán Oíche' ('The Midnight Court') is a sine qua non. Most people too would insist on the inclusion of 'Eibhlín, a Rún', 'Róisín Dhubh', 'Úna Bhán', and of course 'Caoineadh Airt Uí Laoghaire'. For the later, generally the Anglo-Irish, period, specific items are, perhaps, less mandatory—as long as there is something from the seventeenth and eighteenth-century dramatists, something from Thomas Moore (provided he is not going through one of the periods when he is considered worthy only of derision), something from Synge, from Yeats, and possibly Wilde. Otherwise, it would seem, the world of Irish literature is not merely an oyster but the pint of Guinness that goes with it.

The very nature of the items that must be included poses problems. In the case of the heroic tales, for example, the problems are twofold. First there is the problem of length. In many ways the simplest solution to this would have been to create a specially abridged version; this option would not, however, have been fair to the original: it would have been, in its own right, an original composition, giving the bones of the story but little, if any, of its special flavour. There then follows the problem of translation. Totally scholarly translations can be a little arid; unscholarly translations, on the other hand, can be wildly inaccurate. This problem is compounded in translations of poetry. Thomas Moore remarked of the difficulties of translating a particular poem: 'There are no words in the English language capable of doing justice to the Irish.' Finally, of course, it boils down to the simple question, 'What translations are available?' and choosing whichever appears to be most suitable.

A different problem is encountered in choosing extracts from plays or novels. Virtually by definition, both develop their themes over several hundred pages or in the course of an hour or more of actors' time. It is difficult, therefore, to cut out a short passage that does justice to the entire work. The solution here has been to choose a passage that relates to the theme of this book.

Finally there is the problem of songs, the words alone of which do little justice to their musical content. The only solution to this is to point out that there exist recordings of many of the songs contained in this book. Gráinne Yeats, for example, has recorded 'Eibhlín, a Rún' and 'Róisín Dhubh', while Máire Áine Ní Dhonnchadha has recorded notable versions of, for example, 'Úna Bhán' and 'Dónall Óg'.

My mode of selection has been quite simple: if I liked it and it seemed good, it went in. For more recent times there is a natural tendency to include the work of writers who are friends: I plead guilty to this charge, if only on the ground that in many instances their work has become an integral part of my own personal culture. When all is said and done, however, not all of Irish literature can go in, nor can all Irish authors be included; eventually it boils down to a problem that many of the authors included would find comprehensible: you can admire members of the opposite sex in abstract, in general, in vast numbers even, but you cannot possibly have a 'relationship' with all of them, or even the majority of them. Indeed, the world (and his or her spouse) being what they are, to claim that you had even essayed this would attract the maximum of censure—and not a little jealousy. I have, therefore, been content to include those things that I personally admire, even at the expense of things and authors that other people admire greatly. (It was never intended to be a pornographic and yet academic history of Irish literature.)

One point needs specific attention. The fact that part 1, 'From the Irish', terminates in the nineteenth century is not to be taken as a suggestion that writing in Irish also terminated then. Far from it: there is much admirable recent, indeed very recent, writing in Irish. It is not commonly available, however, in translation. As far as the time span of two thousand years is concerned, while it is true that items like the Deirdre story are preserved in manuscripts, such as the Book of Leinster, dated to no earlier that the twelfth century, it is generally and traditionally agreed that the Ulster Cycle in particular reflects a society of the Earlier (pre-Christian) Iron Age, about two thousand years ago. As far as the other end is concerned, there are items included on which the ink is scarcely dry.

Finally, I can only hope that readers derive as much pleasure from reading this collection as I derived from compiling it.

PART ONE

From the Irish

The Exile of the Sons of Uisneach

This is probably the best-known story in Irish literature and has been consistently popular from the date of its composition to the present day. There are two main versions; the earlier one is preserved in three manuscripts, of which that in the Book of Leinster, dated approximately to the middle of the twelfth century, is probably the earliest. It is this version, translated by A. H. Leahy in 1909, that is given below.

In the house of Feidlimid, the son of Dall, even he who was the narrator of stories to Conor the king, the men of Ulster sat at their ale; and before the men, in order to attend upon them, stood the wife of Feidlimid, and she was great with child. Round about the board went drinking-horns, and portions of food; and the revellers shouted in their drunken mirth. And when the men desired to lay themselves down to sleep, the woman also went to her couch; and, as she passed through the midst of the house, the child cried out in her womb, so that its shriek was heard throughout the whole house, and throughout the outer court that lay about it. And upon that shriek, all the men sprang up; and, head closely packed by head, they thronged together in the house, whereupon Sencha, the son of Ailill, rebuked them: 'Let none of you stir!' cried he, 'and let the woman be brought before us, that we may learn what is the meaning of that cry.' Then they brought the woman before them, and thus spoke to her Feidlimid, her spouse:

What is that, of all cries far the fiercest,
    In thy womb raging loudly and long?
Through all ears with that clamour thou piercest;
    With that scream, from sides swollen and strong:

Of great woe, for that cry, is foreboding my heart;
That is torn through with terror, and sore with the smart.

Then the woman turned her, and she approached Cathbad the Druid,
for he was a man of knowledge, and thus she spoke to him:

Give thou ear to me, Cathbad, thou fair one of face,
Thou great crown of our honour, and royal in race;
Let the man so exalted still higher be set,
Let the Druid draw knowledge, that Druids can get.
For I want words of wisdom, and none can I fetch;
Nor to Felim a torch of sure knowledge can stretch:
As no wit of a woman can wot what she bears,
I know naught of that cry from within me that tears.

And then said Cathbad:

'Tis a maid who screamed wildly so lately,
    Fair and curling shall locks round her flow,
And her eyes be blue-centred and stately;
    And her cheeks, like the foxglove, shall glow.
For the tint of her skin, we commend her,
    In its whiteness, like snow newly shed;
And her teeth are all faultless in splendour;
    And her lips, like to coral, are red:
A fair woman is she, for whom heroes, that fight
In their chariots for Ulster, to death shall be dight.

'Tis a woman that shriek who hath given,
    Golden-haired, with long tresses, and tall;
For whose love many chiefs shall have striven,
    And great kings for her favours shall call.
To the west she shall hasten, beguiling
    A great host, that from Ulster shall steal:
Red as coral, her lips shall be smiling,
    As her teeth, white as pearls, they reveal:
Aye, that woman is fair, and great queens shall be fain
Of her form, that is faultless, unflawed by a stain.

Then Cathbad laid his hand upon the body of the woman; and the little child moved beneath his hand: 'Aye, indeed,' he said, 'it is a woman child who is here: Deirdre shall be her name, and evil woe shall be upon her.'

Now some days after that came the girl child into the world; and then thus sang Cathbad:

O Deirdre! of ruin great cause thou art;
    Though famous, and fair, and pale:
Ere that Félim's hid daughter from life shall part,
    All Ulster her deeds shall wail.

Aye, mischief shall come, in the after-time,
    Thou fair shining maid, for thee;
Hear ye this: Usna's sons, the three chiefs sublime,
    To banishment forced shall be.

While thou art in life, shall a fierce wild deed
    In Emain, though late, be done:
Later yet, it shall mourn it refused to heed
    The guard of Róg's powerful son.

O lady of worth! 'tis to thee we owe
    That Fergus to exile flies;
That a son of king Conor we hail in woe,
    When Fiachna is hurt, and dies.

O lady of worth! 'tis all thine the guilt!
    Gerrc, Illadan's son, is slain;
And when Eogan mac Doorha's great life is spilt,
    Not less shall be found our pain.

Grim deed shalt thou do, and in wrath shalt rave
    Against glorious Ulster's king:
In that spot shall men dig thee thy tiny grave;
    Of Deirdre they long shall sing.

'Let that maiden be slain!' cried out the young men of Ulster; but 'Not so!' said Conor; 'she shall in the morning be brought to me, and shall be reared according to my will, and she shall be my wife, and in my companionship shall she dwell.'

The men of Ulster were not so hardy as to turn him from his purpose, and thus it was done. The maiden was reared in a house that belonged to Conor, and she grew up to be the fairest maid in all Ireland. She was brought up at a distance from the king's court; so that none of the men of Ulster might see her till the time came when she was to share the royal couch: none of mankind was permitted to enter the house where she was reared, save only her foster-father, and her foster-mother; and in addition to these Levorcham, to whom naught could any refuse, for she was a witch.

Now once it chanced upon a certain day in the time of winter that the foster-father of Deirdre had employed himself in skinning a calf upon the snow, in order to prepare a roast for her, and the blood of the calf lay upon the snow, and she saw a black raven who came down to drink it. And 'Levorcham,' said Deirdre, 'that man only will I love, who hath the three colours that I see here, his hair as black as the raven, his cheeks red like the blood, and his body as white as the snow.' 'Dignity and good fortune to thee!' said Levorcham; 'that man is not far away. Yonder is he in the burg which is nigh; and the name of him is Naisi, the son of Usnach.' 'I shall never be in good health again,' said Deirdre, 'until the time come when I may see him.'

It befell that Naisi was upon a certain day alone upon the rampart of the burg of Emain, and he sent his warrior-cry with music abroad: well did the musical cry ring out that was raised by the sons of Usnach. Each cow and every beast that heard them, gave of milk two-thirds more than its wont; and each man by whom that cry was heard deemed it to be fully joyous, and a dear pleasure to him. Goodly moreover was the play that these men made with their weapons; if the whole province of Ulster had been assembled together against them in one place, and they three only had been able to set their backs against one another, the men of Ulster would not have borne away victory from those three: so well were they skilled in parry and defence. And they were swift of foot when they hunted the game, and with them it was the custom to chase the quarry to its death.

Now when this Naisi found himself alone on the plain, Deirdre also soon escaped outside her house to him, and she ran past him, and at first he knew not who she might be.

'Fair is the young heifer that springs past me!' he cried.

'Well may the young heifers be great,' she said, 'in a place where none may find a bull.'

'Thou hast, as thy bull,' said he, 'the bull of the whole province of Ulster, even Conor the king of Ulster.'

'I would choose between you two,' she said, 'and I would take for myself a younger bull, even such as thou art.'

'Not so, indeed,' said Naisi, 'for I fear the prophecy of Cathbad.'

'Sayest thou this, as meaning to refuse me?' said she.

'Yea indeed,' he said; and she sprang upon him, and she seized him by his two ears. 'Two ears of shame and of mockery shalt thou have,' she cried, 'if thou take me not with thee.'

'Release me, O my wife!' said he.

'That will I.'

Then Naisi raised his musical warrior-cry, and the men of Ulster heard it, and each of them one after another sprang up: and the sons of Usnach hurried out in order to hold back their brother.

'What is it,' they said, 'that thou dost? let it not be any fault of thine that war is stirred up between us and the men of Ulster.'

Then he told them all that had been done; and 'There shall evil come on thee from this,' said they; 'moreover thou shalt lie under the reproach of shame so long as thou dost live; and we will go with her into another land, for there is no king in all Ireland who will refuse us welcome if we come to him.'

Then they took counsel together, and that same night they departed, three times fifty warriors, and the same number of women, and dogs, and servants, and Deirdre went with them. And for a long time they wandered about Ireland, in homage to this man or that; and often Conor sought to slay them, either by ambuscade or by treachery; from round about Assaroe, near to Ballyshannon in the west, they journeyed, and they turned them back to Benn Etar, in the north-east, which men to-day call the Mountain of Howth. Nevertheless the men of Ulster drave them from the land, and they came to the land of Alba, and in its wildernesses they dwelled. And when the chase of the wild beasts of the mountains failed them, they made foray upon the cattle of the men of Alba, and took them for themselves; and the men of Alba gathered themselves together with intent to destroy them. Then they took shelter with the king of Alba, and the king took them into

his following, and they served him in war. And they made for themselves houses of their own in the meadows by the king's burg; it was
on account of Deirdre that these houses were made, for they feared
that men might see her, and that on her account they might be slain.

Now one day the high-steward of the king went out in the early
morning, and he made a cast about Naisi's house, and saw those two
sleeping therein, and he hurried back to the king, and awaked him:
'We have,' said he, 'up to this day found no wife for thee of like dignity to thyself. Naisi the son of Usnach hath a wife of worth sufficient
for the emperor of the western world! Let Naisi be slain, and let his
wife share thy couch.'

'Not so!' said the king, 'but do thou prepare thyself to go each
day to her house, and woo her for me secretly.'

Thus was it done; but Deirdre, whatsoever the steward told her,
was accustomed straightway to recount it each even to her spouse;
and since nothing was obtained from her, the sons of Usnach were
sent into dangers, and into wars, and into strifes that thereby they
might be overcome. Nevertheless they showed themselves to be
stout in every strife, so that no advantage did the king gain from them
by such attempts as these.

The men of Alba were gathered together to destroy the sons of
Usnach, and this also was told to Deirdre. And she told her news to
Naisi: 'Depart hence!' said she, 'for if ye depart not this night, upon
the morrow ye shall be slain!' And they marched away that night, and
they betook themselves to an island of the sea.

Now the news of what had passed was brought to the men of
Ulster. ''Tis pity, O Conor!' said they, 'that the sons of Usnach
should die in the land of foes, for the sake of an evil woman. It is better that they should come under thy protection, and that the (fated)
slaying should be done here, and that they should come into their
own land, rather than that they should fall at the hands of foes.' 'Let
them come to us then,' said Conor, 'and let men go as securities to
them.' The news was brought to them.

'This is welcome news for us,' they said; 'we will indeed come,
and let Fergus come as our surety, and Dubhtach, and Cormac the
son of Conor.' These then went to them, and they moved them to
pass over the sea.

6

But at the contrivance of Conor, Fergus was pressed to join in an ale-feast, while the sons of Usnach were pledged to eat no food in Erin, until they had eaten the food of Conor. So Fergus tarried behind with Dubhtach and Cormac; and the sons of Usnach went on, accompanied by Fiacha, Fergus' son; until they came to the meadows around Emain.

Now at that time Eogan the son of Durthacht had come to Emain to make his peace with Conor, for they had for a long time been at enmity; and to him, and to the warmen of Conor, the charge was given that they should slay the sons of Usnach, in order that they should not come before the king. The sons of Usnach stood upon the level part of the meadows, and the women sat upon the ramparts of Emain. And Eogan came with his warriors across the meadow, and the son of Fergus took his place by Naisi's side. And Eogan greeted them with a mighty thrust of his spear, and the spear brake Naisi's back in sunder, and passed through it. The son of Fergus made a spring, and he threw both arms around Naisi, and he brought him beneath himself to shelter him, while he threw himself down above him; and it was thus that Naisi was slain, through the body of the son of Fergus. Then there began a murder throughout the meadow, so that none escaped who did not fall by the points of the spears, or the edge of the sword, and Deirdre was brought to Conor to be in his power, and her arms were bound behind her back.

Now the sureties who had remained behind, heard what had been done, even Fergus and Dubhtach, and Cormac. And thereon they hastened forward, and they forthwith performed great deeds. Dubhtach slew, with the one thrust of his spear, Mane a son of Conor, and Fiachna the son of Feidelm, Conor's daughter; and Fergus struck down Traigthren, the son of Traiglethan, and his brother. And Conor was wrath at this, and he came to the fight with them; so that upon that day three hundred of the men of Ulster fell. And Dubhtach slew the women of Ulster; and, ere the day dawned, Fergus set Emain on fire. Then they went away into exile, and betook them to the land of Connaught to find shelter with Ailill and Maev, for they knew that that royal pair would give them good entertainment. To the men of Ulster the exiles showed no love: three thousand stout men went with them; and for sixteen years never did they allow cries of

lamentation and of fear among the Ulstermen to cease: each night
their vengeful forays caused men to quake, and to wail.

Deirdre lived on for a year in the household of Conor; and during
all that time she smiled no smile of laughter; she satisfied not herself
with food or with sleep, and she raised not her head from her knee.
And if any one brought before her people of mirth, she used to speak
thus:

> Though eager troops, and fair to see,
>   May home return, though these ye wait:
> When Usna's sons came home to me,
>   They came with more heroic state.
>
> With hazel mead, my Naisi stood:
>   And near our fire his bath I'd pour;
> On Aindle's stately back the wood;
>   On Ardan's ox, or goodly boar.
>
> Though sweet that goodly mead ye think
>   That warlike Conor drinks in hall,
> I oft have known a sweeter drink,
>   Where leaps in foam the waterfall:
>
> Our board was spread beneath the tree,
>   And Naisi raised the cooking flame:
> More sweet than honey-sauced to me
>   Was meat, prepared from Naisi's game.
>
> Though well your horns may music blow,
>   Though sweet each month your pipes may sound,
> I fearless say, that well I know
>   A sweeter strain I oft have found.
>
> Though horns and pipes be sounding clear,
>   Though Conor's mind in these rejoice,
> More magic strain, more sweet, more dear
>   Was Usna's Children's noble voice.

Like sound of wave, rolled Naisi's bass;
  We'd hear him long, so sweet he sang:
And Ardan's voice took middle place;
  And clearly Aindle's tenor rang.

Now Naisi lies within his tomb:
  A sorry guard his friends supplied;
His kindred poured his cup of doom,
  That poisoned cup, by which he died.

Ah! Berthan dear! thy lands are fair;
  Thy men are proud, though hills be stern:
Alas! to-day I rise not there
  To wait for Usna's sons' return.

That firm, just mind, so loved, alas!
  The dear shy youth, with touch of scorn,
I loved with him through woods to pass,
  And girding in the early morn.

When bent on foes, they boded ill,
  Those dear grey eyes, that maids adored;
When, spent with toil, his troops lay still,
  Through Irish woods his tenor soared.

For this it is, no more I sleep;
  No more my nails with pink I stain:
No joy can break the watch I keep;
  For Usna's sons come not again.

For half the night no sleep I find;
  No couch can me to rest beguile:
'Mid crowds of thoughts still strays my mind;
  I find no time to eat or smile.

In eastern Emain's proud array
  No time to joy is left for me;
For gorgeous house, and garments gay,
  Nor peace, nor joy, nor rest can be.

And when Conor sought to soothe her, thus Deirdre would answer him:

Ah Conor! what of thee? I naught can do!
    Lament and sorrow on my life have passed:
The ill you fashioned lives my whole life through;
    A little time your love for me would last.

The man to me most fair beneath the sky,
    The man I loved, in death away you tore:
The crime you did was great; for, till I die,
    That face I loved I never shall see more.

That he is gone is all my sorrow still;
    Before me looms the shape of Usna's son;
Though o'er his body white is yon dark hill,
    There's much I'd lavish, if but him I won.

I see his cheeks, with meadow's blush they glow;
    Black as a beetle, runs his eyebrows' line;
His lips are red; and, white as noble snow
    I see his teeth, like pearls they seem to shine.

Well have I known the splendid garb he bears,
    Oft among Alba's warriors seen of old:
A crimson mantle, such as courtier wears,
    And edged with border wrought of ruddy gold.

Of silk his tunic; great its costly price;
    For full one hundred pearls thereon are sewn;
Stitched with *findruine*, bright with strange device,
    Full fifty ounces weighed those threads alone.

Gold-hilted in his hand I see his sword;
    Two spears he holds, with spear-heads grim and green;
Around his shield the yellow gold is poured,
    And in its midst a silver boss is seen.

Fair Fergus ruin on us all hath brought!
　　We crossed the ocean, and to him gave heed:
His honour by a cup of ale was bought;
　　From him hath passed the fame of each high deed.

If Ulster on this plain were gathered here
　　Before king Conor; and those troops he'd give,
I'd lose them all, nor think the bargain dear,
　　If I with Naisi, Usna's son, could live.

Break not, O king, my heart to-day in me;
　　For soon, though young, I come my grave unto:
My grief is stronger than the strength of sea;
　　Thou, Conor, knowest well my word is true.

'Whom dost thou hate the most,' said Conor, 'of these whom thou now seest?'

'Thee thyself,' she answered, 'and with thee Eogan the son of Durthacht.'

'Then,' said Conor, 'thou shalt dwell with Eogan for a year;' and he gave Deirdre over into Eogan's hand.

Now upon the morrow they went away over the festal plain of Macha, and Deirdre sat behind Eogan in the chariot; and the two who were with her were the two men whom she would never willingly have seen together upon the earth, and as she looked upon them. 'Ha, Deirdre,' said Conor, 'it is the same glance that a ewe gives when between two rams that thou sharest now between me and Eogan!' Now there was a great rock of stone in front of them, and Deirdre struck her head upon that stone, and she shattered her head, and so she died.

This then is the tale of the exile of the sons of Usnach, and of the Exile of Fergus, and of the death of Deirdre.

Deirdre's Lament for the Sons of Uisneach

*This is a translation of a variant form of 'Deirdre's Lament
for the Sons of Uisneach', which does not appear in the version
of the Book of Leinster but does appear in later versions of the
tale, translated by Sir Samuel Ferguson.*

The lions of the hill are gone,
And I am left alone—alone—
Dig the grave both wide and deep,
For I am sick, and fain would sleep!

The falcons of the wood are flown,
And I am left alone—alone—
Dig the grave both deep and wide,
And let us slumber side by side.

The dragons of the rock are sleeping,
Sleep that wakes not for our weeping:
Dig the grave and make it ready;
Lay me on my true Love's body.

Lay their spears and bucklers bright
By the warriors' sides aright;
Many a day the Three before me
On their linkèd bucklers bore me.

Lay upon the low grave floor,
'Neath each head, the blue claymore;
Many a time the noble Three
Redden'd those blue blades for me.

Lay the collars, as is meet,
Of their greyhounds at their feet;
Many a time for me have they
Brought the tall red deer to bay.

Oh! to hear my true Love singing,
Sweet as sound of trumpets ringing:
Like the sway of ocean swelling
Roll'd his deep voice round our dwelling.

Oh! to hear the echoes pealing
Round our green and fairy sheeling,
When the Three, with soaring chorus,
Pass'd the silent skylark o'er us.

Echo now, sleep, morn and even—
Lark alone enchant the heaven!—
Ardan's lips are scant of breath,—
Neesa's tongue is cold in death.

Stag, exult on glen and mountain—
Salmon, leap from loch to fountain—
Heron, in the free air warm ye—
Usnach's Sons no more will harm ye!

Erin's stay no more you are,
Rulers of the ridge of war;
Never more 'twill be your fate
To keep the beam of battle straight.

Woe is me! by fraud and wrong—
Traitors false and tyrants strong—
Fell Clan Usnach, bought and sold,
For Barach's feast and Conor's gold!

Woe to Eman, roof and wall!—
Woe to Red Branch, hearth and hall!—
Tenfold woe and black dishonour
To the false and four Clan Conor!

Dig the grave both wide and deep,
Sick I am, and fain would sleep!
Dig the grave and make it ready,
Lay me on my true Love's body.

The Wooing of Eimhear

This is the story of how Cú Chulainn, the Ulster hero,
wooed his bride. It is taken from a version preserved in the
Stowe manuscript, given by Eleanor Hull in her
Cuchulain: the Hound of Ulster *(1909).*

It was on a day of the days of summer that Emer, daughter of Forgall the Wily, sat on a bench before her father's door, at his fort that is called Lusk to-day, but which in olden days men spoke of as the Gardens of the Sun-god Lugh, so sunny and so fair and fertile was that plain, with waving meadow-grass and buttercups, and the sweet may-blossom girdling the fields. Close all about the fort the gardens lay, with apple-trees shedding their pink and white upon the playing fields of brilliant green; and all the air was noisy with the buzz of bees, and with the happy piping of the thrush and soft low cooing of the doves. And Emer sat, a fair and noble maid, among her young companions, foster-sisters of her own, who came from all the farms and forts around to grow up with the daughters of the house, and learn from them high-bred and gentle ways, to fashion rich embroideries such as Irish women used to practise as an art, and weaving, and fine needlework, and all the ways of managing a house. And as they sat round Emer, a bright comely group of busy girls, they sang in undertones the crooning tender melodies of ancient Erin; or one would tell a tale of early wars, and warrior feasts or happenings of the gods, and one would tell a tale of lover's joys or of the sorrows of a blighted love, and they would sigh and laugh and dream that they too loved, were wooed, and lost their loves.

And Emer moved about among the girls, directing them; and of all maids in Erin, Emer was the best, for hers were the six gifts of womanhood, the gift of loveliness, the gift of song, the gift of sweet and pleasant speech, the gift of handiwork, the gifts of wisdom and of modesty. And in his distant home in Ulster, Cuchulain heard of her. For he was young and brave, and women loved him for his nobleness, and all men wished that he should take a wife. But for awhile he would not, for among the women whom he saw, not one of them came up to his desires. And when they urged him, wilfully he said: 'Well, find for me a woman I could love, and I will marry her.' Then sent the King his heralds out through every part of Ulster and the south to seek a wife whom Cuchulain would care to woo. But still he said the same, 'This one, and this, has some bad temper or some want of grace, or she is vain or she is weak, not fitted as a mate to such as I. She must be brave, for she must suffer much; she must be gentle, lest I anger her; she must be fair and noble, not alone to give me pleasure as her spouse, but that all men may think of her with pride, saying, "As Cuchulain is the first of Ulster's braves, the hero of her many fighting-fields, so is his wife the noblest and the first of Erin's women, a worthy mate for him."'

So when the princely messengers returned, their search was vain; among the daughters of the chiefs and noble lords not one was found whom Cuchulain cared to woo. But one who loved him told him of a night he spent in Forgall's fort, and of the loveliness and noble spirit of Forgall's second girl Emer, the maiden of the waving hair, but just grown up to womanhood. He told him of her noble mien and stately step, the soft and liquid brightness of her eyes, the colour of her hair, that like to ruddy gold fresh from the burnishing, was rolled around her head. Her graceful form he praised, her skilfulness in song and handiwork, her courage with her father, a harsh and wily man, whom all within the house hated and feared but she. He told him also that for any man to win the maiden for his wife would be a troublesome and dangerous thing, for out of all the world, her father Forgall loved and prized but her, and he had made it known that none beneath a king or ruling prince should marry her, and any man who dared to win her love, but such as these, should meet a cruel death; and this he laid upon his sons and made them swear to him upon their swords, that any who should come to woo the girl should never leave the fort alive again.

All that they said but made Cuchulain yet the more desire to see the maid and talk with her. 'This girl, so brave, so wise, so fair of face and form,' he pondered with himself, 'would be a fitting mate for any chief. I think she is the fitting mate for me.'

So on the very day when Emer sat upon her playing-fields, Cuchulain in the early morn set forth in all his festal garb in his chariot with his prancing steeds, with Laeg before him as his charioteer, and took the shortest route towards the plain of Bray, where lie the Gardens of the Sun-god Lugh. The way they went from Emain lay between the Mountains of the Wood, and thence along the High-road of the Plain, where once the sea had passed; across the marsh that bore the name the Whisper of the Secret of the Gods. Then driving on towards the River Boyne they passed the Ridge of the Great Sow, where not far off is seen the fairy haunt of Angus, God of Beauty and of Youth; and so they reached the ford of Washing of the Horses of the Gods, and the fair, flowering plains of Lugh, called Lusk to-day.

Now all the girls were busied with their work, when on the high-road leading to the fort they heard a sound like thunder from the north, that made them pause and listen in surprise.

Nearer and nearer yet it came as though at furious pace a band of warriors bore down towards the house. 'Let one of you see from the ramparts of the fort,' said Emer, 'what is the sound that we hear coming towards us.' Fiall, her sister, Forgall's eldest girl, ran to the top of the rath or earthen mound that circled round the playing-fields, and looked out towards the north, shading her eyes against the brilliant sun. 'What do you see there?' asked they all, and eagerly she cried: 'I see a splendid chariot-chief coming at furious pace along the road. Two steeds, like day and night, of equal size and beauty, come thundering beneath that chariot on the plain. Curling their manes and long, and as they come, one would think fire darted from their curbed jaws, so strain and bound they forward; high in the air the turf beneath their feet is thrown around them, as though a flock of birds were following as they go. On the right side the horse is grey, broad in the haunches, active, swift and wild; with head erect and breast expanded, madly he moves along the plain, bounding and prancing as he goes. The other horse jet-black, head firmly knit, feet broad-hoofed, firm, and slender; in all this land never had chariot-chief such steeds as these.'

'Heed not the steeds,' the girls replied, 'tell us, for this concerns us most, who is the chariot-chief who rides within?'

'Worthy of the chariot in which he rides is he who sits within. Youthful he seems, as standing on the very borders of a noble manhood, and yet I think his face and form are older than his years. Gravely he looks, as though his mind revolved some serious thought, and yet a radiance as of the summer's day enfolds him round. About his shoulders a rich five-folded mantle hangs, caught by a brooch across the chest sparkling with precious gems, above his white and gold-embroidered shirt. His massive sword rests on his thigh, and yet I think he comes not here to fight. Before him stands his charioteer, the reins held firmly in his hand, urging the horses onward with a goad.'

'What like is he, the charioteer?' demand the girls again.

'A ruddy man and freckled,' answered Fiall; 'his hair is very curly and bright-red, held by a bronze fillet across his brow, and caught at either side his head in little cups of gold, to keep the locks from falling on his face. A light cloak on his shoulders, made with open sleeves, flies back in the wind, as rapidly they course along the plain.' But Emer heard not what the maiden said, for to her mind there came the memory of a wondrous youth whom Ulster loved and yet of whom all Erin stood in awe. Great warriors spoke of him in whispers and with shaking of the head. They told how when he was a little child, he fought with full-grown warriors and mastered them; of a huge hound that he had slain and many feats of courage he had done. Into her mind there came a memory, that she had heard of prophets who foretold for him a strange and perilous career; a life of danger, and an early death. Full many a time she longed to see this youth, foredoomed to peril, yet whose praise should ring from age to age through Erin; and in her mind, when all alone she pondered on these things, she still would end: 'This were a worthy mate! This were a man to win a woman's love!' And half aloud she uttered the old words: 'This were a man to win a woman's love!'

Now hardly had the words sprung to her lips, when the chariot stood before the door, close to the place where all the girls were gathered. And when she saw him Emer knew it was the man of whom she dreamed. He wished a blessing to them, and her lovely face she lifted in reply. 'May God make smooth the path before thy feet,' she gently said. 'And thou, mayest thou be safe from every harm,' was his reply. 'Whence comest thou?' she asked; for he had alighted from his seat and stood beside her, gazing on her face. 'From Conor's court we come,' he answered then; 'from Emain, kingliest of Ulster's forts, and this the way we took. We drove between the Mountains of the Wood, along the High-road of the Plain, where once the sea had been; across the Marsh they call the Secret of the Gods, and to the Boyne's ford named of old the Washing of the Horses of the Gods. And now at last, O maiden, we have come to the bright flowery Garden-grounds of Lugh. This is the story of myself, O maid; let me now hear of thee.' Then Emer said: 'Daughter am I to Forgall, whom men call the Wily Chief. Cunning his mind and strange his powers; for he is stronger than any labouring man, more learned than any Druid, more sharp and clever than any man of verse. Men say that thou art skilled in feats of war, but it will be more than all thy games to fight against Forgall himself; therefore be cautious what thou doest, for men cannot number the multitude of his warlike deeds nor the cunning and craft with which he works. He has given me as a bodyguard twenty valiant men, their captain Con, son of Forgall, and my brother; therefore I am well protected, and no man can come near me, but that Forgall knows of it. To-day he is gone from home on a warrior expedition, and those men are gone with him; else, had he been within, I trow he would have asked thee of thy business here.'

'Why, O maiden, dost thou talk thus to me? Dost thou not reckon me among the strong men, who know not fear?' 'If thy deeds were known to me,' she said, 'I then might reckon them; but hitherto I have not heard of all thy exploits.' 'Truly, I swear, O maiden,' said Cuchulain, 'that I will make my deeds to be recounted among the glories of the warrior-feats of heroes.' 'How do men reckon thee?' she said again. 'What then is thy strength?' 'This is my strength,' he said. 'When my might in fight is weakest, I can defend myself alone against twenty. I fear not by my own might to fight with forty. Under my protection a hundred are secure. From dread of me, strong warriors avoid my path, and come not against me in the battle-field. Hosts and multitudes and armed men fly before my name.'

'Thou seemest to boast,' said Emer, 'and truly for a tender boy those feats are very good; but they rank not with the deeds of chariot-chiefs. Who then were they who brought thee up in these deeds of which thou boastest?'

'Truly, O maiden, King Conor is himself my foster-father, and not as a churl or common man was I brought up by him. Among chariot-chiefs and champions, among poets and learned men, among the lords and nobles of Ulster, have I been reared, and they have taught me courage and skill and manly gifts. In birth and bravery I am a match for any chariot-chief; I direct the counsels of Ulster, and at my own fort at Dun Dalgan they come to me for entertainment. Not as one of the common herd do I stand before thee here to-day, but as the favourite of the King and the darling of all the warriors of Ulster. Moreover, the god Lugh the Long-handed is my protector, for I am of the race of the great gods, and his especial foster-child. And now, O maiden, tell me of thyself; how in the sunny plains of Lugh hast thou been reared within thy father's fort?' 'That I will tell thee,' said the girl. 'I was brought up in noble behaviour as every queen is reared; in stateliness of form, in wise, calm speech, in comeliness of manner, so that to me is imputed every noble grace among the hosts of the women of Erin.'

'Good, indeed, are those virtues,' said the youth; 'and yet I see one excellence thou hast not noted in thy speech. Never before, until this day, among all women with whom I have at times conversed, have I found one but thee to speak the mystic ancient language of the bards, which we are talking now for secrecy one with the other. And all these things are good, but one is best of all, and that is, that I love thee, and I think thou lovest me. What hinders, then, that we should be betrothed?' But Emer would not hasten, but teasing him, she said, 'Perhaps thou hast already found a wife?' 'Not so,' said he, 'and by my right-hand's valour here I vow, none but thyself shall ever be my wife.' 'A pity it were, indeed, thou shouldst not have a wife,' said Emer, playing with him still; 'see, here is Fiall, my elder sister, a clever girl and excellent in needlework. Make her thy wife, for well is it known to thee, a younger sister in Ireland may not marry before an elder. Take her! I'll call her hither.' Then Cuchulain was vexed because she seemed to play with him. 'Verily and indeed,' he said, 'not Fiall, but thee, it is with whom I am in love; and if thou weddest me not, never will I, Cuchulain, wed at all.'

Then Emer saw that Cuchulain loved her, but she was not satisfied, because he had not yet done the deeds of prime heroes, and she desired that he should prove himself by champion feats and deeds of valour before he won her as his bride.

So she bade him go away and prove himself for a year by deeds of prowess to be indeed a worthy mate and spouse for her, and then, if he would come again she would go with him as his one and only wife. But she bade him beware of her father, for she knew that he would try to kill him, in order that he might not come again. And this was true, for every way he sought to kill Cuchulain, or to have him killed by his enemies, but he did not prevail.

When Cuchulain had taken farewell of Emer and gained her promise, he returned to Emain Macha. And that night the maidens of the fort told Forgall that Cuchulain had been there and that they thought that he had come to woo Emer; but of this they were not sure, because he and Emer had talked together in the poet's mystic tongue, that was not known to them. For Emer and Cuchulain talked on this wise, that no one might repeat what they had said to Forgall.

And for a whole year Cuchulain was away, and Forgall guarded the fort so well that he could not come near Emer to speak with her; but at last, when the year was out, he would wait no longer, and he wrote a message to Emer on a piece of stick, telling her to be ready. And he came in his war-chariot, with scythes upon its wheels, and he brought a band of hardy men with him, who entered the outer rampart of the fort and carried off Emer, striking down men on every side. And Forgall followed them to the earthen out-works, but he fell over the rath, and was taken up lifeless. And Cuchulain placed Emer and her foster-sister in his chariot, carrying with them their garments and ornaments of gold and silver, and they drove northward to Cuchulain's fort at Dun Dalgan, which is Dundalk to-day.

And they were pursued to the Boyne, and there Cuchulain placed Emer in a house of safety, and he turned and drove off his enemies who followed him, pursuing them along the banks and destroying them, so that the place, which had before been called the White Field, was called the Turf of Blood from that day. Then he and Emer reached their home in safety, nor were they henceforth parted until death.

The Wooing of Éadaoin

*This is another 'wooing' story; in this case the wooer is
Eochaidh and the wooed is Éadaoin. The translation is that
published in 1905 by A. H. Leahy.*

E ochaid Airemon took the sovereignty over Erin, and the five
provinces of Ireland were obedient to him, for the king of
each province was his vassal. Now these were they who were
the kings of the provinces at that time, even Conor the son of Ness,
and Messgegra, and Tigernach Tetbannach, and Curoi, and Ailill the
son of Mata of Muresc. And the royal forts that belonged to Eochaid
were the stronghold of Frémain in Meath, and the stronghold of
Frémain in Tethba; moreover the stronghold of Frémain in Tethba
was more pleasing to him than any other of the forts of Erin.

Now a year after that Eochaid had obtained the sovereignty, he
sent out his commands to the men of Ireland that they should come
to Tara to hold festival therein, in order that there should be adjusted
the taxes and the imposts that should be set upon them, so that these
might be settled for a period of five years. And the one answer that
the men of Ireland made to Eochaid was that they would not make
for the king that assembly which is the Festival of Tara until he
found for himself a queen, for there was no queen to stand by the
king's side when Eochaid first assumed the kingdom.

Then Eochaid sent out the messengers of each of the five
provinces to go through the land of Ireland to seek for that woman or
girl who was the fairest to be found in Erin; and he bade them to note
that no woman should be to him as a wife, unless she had never before
been as a wife to any one of the men of the land. And at the Bay of
Cichmany a wife was found for him, and her name was Etain, the
daughter of Etar; and Eochaid brought her thereafter to his palace, for
she was a wife meet for him, by reason of her form, and her beauty,
and her descent, and her brilliancy, and her youth, and her renown.

Now Finn the son of Findloga had three sons, all sons of a queen, even Eochaid Fedlech, and Eochaid Airemm, and Ailill Anguba. And Ailill Anguba was seized with love for Etain at the Festival of Tara, after that she had been wedded to Eochaid; since he for a long time gazed upon her. And, since such gazing is a token of love, Ailill gave much blame to himself for the deed that he was doing, yet it helped him not. For his longing was too strong for his endurance, and for this cause he fell into a sickness; and, that there might be no stain upon his honour, his sickness was concealed by him from all, neither did he speak of it to the lady herself. Then Fachtna, the chief physician of Eochaid, was brought to look upon Ailill, when it was understood that his death might be near, and thus the physician spoke to him: 'One of the two pangs that slay a man, and for which there is no healing by leechcraft, is upon thee; either the pangs of envy or the pangs of love.' And Ailill refused to confess the cause of his illness to the physician, for he was withheld by shame; and he was left behind in Frémain of Tethba to die; and Eochaid went upon his royal progress throughout all Erin, and he left Etain behind him to be near Ailill, in order that the last rites of Ailill might be done by her; that she might cause his grave to be dug, and that the keen might be raised for him, and that his cattle should be slain for him as victims. And to the house where Ailill lay in his sickness went Etain each day to converse with him, and his sickness was eased by her presence; and, so long as Etain was in that place where he was, so long was he accustomed to gaze at her.

Now Etain observed all this, and she bent her mind to discover the cause, and one day when they were in the house together, Etain asked of Ailill what was the cause of his sickness. 'My sickness,' said Ailill, 'comes from my love for thee.' ''Tis pity,' said she, 'that thou hast so long kept silence, for thou couldest have been healed long since, had we but known of its cause.' 'And even now could I be healed,' said Ailill, 'did I but find favour in thy sight.' 'Thou shalt find favour,' she said. Each day after they had spoken thus with each other, she came to him for the fomenting of his head, and for the giving of the portion of food that was required by him, and for the pouring of water over his hands; and three weeks after that, Ailill was whole. Then he said to Etain: 'Yet is the completion of my cure at thy hands lacking to me; when may it be that I shall have it?' ''Tis to-morrow it shall be,' she answered him, 'but it shall not be in the abode of the lawful monarch of the land that this felony shall be done. Thou shalt come,' she said, 'on the morrow to yonder hill that riseth beyond the fort: there shall be the tryst that thou desirest.'

Now Ailill lay awake all that night, and he fell into a sleep at the hour when he should have kept his tryst, and he woke not from his sleep until the third hour of the day. And Etain went to her tryst and she saw a man before her; like was his form to the form of Ailill, he lamented the weakness that his sickness had caused him, and he gave to her such answers as it was fitting that Ailill should give. But at the third hour of the day, Ailill himself awoke: and he had for a long time remained in sorrow when Etain came into the house where he was; and as she approached him, 'What maketh thee so sorrowful?' said Etain. ''Tis because thou wert sent to tryst with me,' said Ailill, 'and I came not to thy presence, and sleep fell upon me, so that I have but now awakened from it; and surely my chance of being healed hath now gone from me.' 'Not so, indeed,' answered Etain, 'for there is a morrow to follow to-day.' And upon that night he took his watch with a great fire before him, and with water beside him to put upon his eyes.

At the hour that was appointed for the tryst, Etain came for her meeting with Ailill, and she saw the same man, like unto Ailill, whom she had seen before; and Etain went to the house, and saw Ailill still lamenting. And Etain came three times, and yet Ailill kept not his tryst, and she found that same man there every time. ''Tis not for thee,' she said, 'that I came to this tryst: why comest thou to meet me? And as for him whom I would have met, it was for no sin or evil desire that I came to meet him; but it was fitting for the wife of the king of Ireland to rescue the man from the sickness under which he hath so long been oppressed.' 'It were more fitting for thee to tryst with me myself,' said the man, 'for when thou wert Etain of the Horses, the daughter of Ailill, it was I who was thy husband. And when thou camest to be wife to me, thou didst leave a great price behind thee; even a marriage price of the chief plains and waters of Ireland, and as much of gold and of silver as might match thee in value.' 'Why,' said she, 'what is thy name?' ''Tis easy to say,' he answered; 'Mider of Bri Leith is my name.' 'Truly,' said she; 'and what was the cause that parted us?' 'That also is easy,' he said; 'it was the sorcery of Fuamnach, and the spells of Bressal Etarlam.' And then Mider said to Etain:

Wilt thou come to my home, fair-haired lady? to dwell
In the marvellous land of the musical spell,
Where the crowns of all heads are, as primroses, bright,
And from head to the heel all men's bodies snow-white.

In that land of no 'mine' nor of 'thine' is there speech,
But their teeth flashing white and dark eyebrows hath each;
In all eyes shine our hosts, as reflected they swarm,
And each cheek with the pink of the foxglove is warm.

With the heather's rich tint every blushing neck glows,
In our eyes are all shapes that the blackbird's egg shows;
And the plains of thine Erin, though pleasing to see,
When the Great Plain is sighted, as deserts shall be.

Though ye think the ale strong in the Island of Fate,
Yet they drink it more strong in the Land of the Great;
Of a country where marvel abounds have I told,
Where no young man in rashness thrusts backward the old.

There are streams smooth and luscious that flow through
    that land,
And of mead and of wine is the best at each hand;
And of crime there is naught the whole country within,
There are men without blemish, and love without sin.

Through the world of mankind, seeing all, can we float,
And yet none, though we see them, their see-ers can note;
For the sin of their sire is a mist on them flung,
None may count up our host who from Adam is sprung.

Lady, come to that folk; to that strong folk of mine;
And with gold on thy head thy fair tresses shall shine:
'Tis on pork the most dainty that then thou shalt feed,
And for drink have thy choice of new milk and of mead.

'I will not come with thee,' answered Etain, 'I will not give up the king of Ireland for thee, a man who knows not his own clan nor his kindred.' 'It was indeed myself,' said Mider, 'who long ago put beneath the mind of Ailill the love that he hath felt for thee, so that his blood ceased to run, and his flesh fell away from him: it was I also who have taken away his desire, so that there might be no hurt to thine honour. But wilt thou come with me to my land,' said Mider, 'in case Eochaid should ask it of thee?' 'I would come in such case,' answered to him Etain.

After all this Etain departed to the house. 'It hath indeed been good, this our tryst,' said Ailill, 'for I have been cured of my sickness; moreover, in no way has thine honour been stained.' ''Tis glorious that it hath fallen out so,' answered Etain. And afterwards Eochaid came back from his royal progress, and he was grateful for that his brother's life had been preserved, and he gave all thanks to Etain for the great deed she had done while he was away from his palace.

Now upon another time it chanced that Eochaid Airemm, the king of Tara, arose upon a certain fair day in the time of summer; and he ascended the high ground of Tara to behold the plain of Breg; beautiful was the colour of that plain, and there was upon it excellent blossom, glowing with all hues that are known. And, as the aforesaid Eochaid looked about and around him, he saw a young strange warrior upon the high ground at his side. The tunic that the warrior wore was purple in colour, his hair was of a golden yellow, and of such length that it reached to the edge of his shoulders. The eyes of the young warrior were lustrous and grey; in the one hand he held a five-pointed spear, in the other a shield with a white central boss, and with gems of gold upon it. And Eochaid held his peace, for he knew that none such had been in Tara on the night before, and the gate that led into the *Liss* had not at that hour been thrown open.

The warrior came, and placed himself under the protection of Eochaid; and 'Welcome do I give,' said Eochaid, 'to the hero who is yet unknown.'

'Thy reception is such as I expected when I came,' said the warrior.

'We know thee not,' answered Eochaid.

'Yet thee in truth I know well!' he replied.

'What is the name by which thou are called?' said Eochaid.

'My name is not known to renown,' said the warrior; 'I am Mider of Bri Leith.'

'And for what purpose art thou come?' said Eochaid.

'I have come that I may play a game at the chess with thee,' answered Mider. 'Truly,' said Eochaid, 'I myself am skilful at the chess-play.'

'Let us test that skill!' said Mider.

'Nay,' said Eochaid, 'the queen is even now in her sleep; and hers is the palace in which the chessboard lies.'

'I have here with me,' said Mider, 'a chessboard which is not inferior to thine.' It was even as he said, for that chessboard was silver, and the men to play with were gold; and upon that board were costly stones, casting their light on every side, and the bag that held the men was of woven chains of brass.

Mider then set out the chessboard, and he called upon Eochaid to play. 'I will not play,' said Eochaid, 'unless we play for a stake.'

'What stake shall we have upon the game then?' said Mider.

'It is indifferent to me,' said Eochaid.

'Then,' said Mider, 'if thou dost obtain the forfeit of my stake, I will bestow on thee fifty steeds of a dark grey, their heads of a blood-red colour, but dappled; their ears pricked high, and their chests broad; their nostrils wide, and their hoofs slender; great is their strength, and they are keen like a whetted edge; eager are they, high-standing, and spirited, yet easily stopped in their course.'

Many games were played between Eochaid and Mider; and, since Mider did not put forth his whole strength, the victory on all occasions rested with Eochaid. But instead of the gifts which Mider had offered, Eochaid demanded that Mider and his folk should perform for him services which should be of benefit to his realm; that he should clear away the rocks and stones from the plains of Meath, should remove the rushes which made the land barren around his favourite fort of Tethba, should cut down the forest of Breg, and finally should build a causeway across the moor or bog of Lamrach that men might pass freely across it. All these things Mider agreed to do, and Eochaid sent his steward to see how that work was done. And when it came to the time after sunset, the steward looked, and he saw that Mider and his fairy host, together with fairy oxen, were labouring at the causeway over the bog; and thereupon much of earth and of gravel and of stones was poured into it. Now it had, before that time, always been the custom of the men of Ireland to harness their oxen with a strap over their foreheads, so that the pull might be against the foreheads of the oxen; and this custom lasted up to that very night, when it was seen that the fairy-folk had placed the yoke upon the shoulders of the oxen, so that the pull might be there; and in this way were the yokes of the oxen afterwards placed by Eochaid, and thence cometh the name by which he is known; even Eochaid Airemm, or Eochaid the Ploughman, for he was the first of all the men of Ireland to put the yokes on the necks of the oxen, and thus it became the custom for all the land of Ireland. And this is the song that the host of the fairies sang, as they laboured at the making of the road:

> Thrust it in hand! force it in hand!
> Nobles this night, as an ox-troop, stand:
> Hard is the task that is asked, and who
> From the bridging of Lamrach shall gain, or rue?

Not in all the world could a road have been found that should be better than the road that they made, had it not been that the fairy folk were observed as they worked upon it; but for that cause a breach hath been made in that causeway. And the steward of Eochaid thereafter came to him; and he described to him that great labouring band that had come before his eyes, and he said that there was not over the chariot-pole of life a power that could withstand its might. And, as they spake thus with each other, they saw Mider standing before them; high was he girt, and ill-favoured was the face that he showed; and Eochaid arose, and he gave welcome to him. 'Thy welcome is such as I expected when I came,' said Mider. 'Cruel and senseless hast thou been in thy treatment of me, and much of hardship and suffering hast thou given me. All things that seemed good in thy sight have I got for thee, but now anger against thee hath filled my mind!' 'I return not anger for anger,' answered Eochaid; 'what thou wishest shall be done.' 'Let it be as thou wishest,' said Mider; 'shall we play at the chess?' said he. 'What stake shall we set upon the game?' said Eochaid. 'Even such stake as the winner of it shall demand,' said Mider. And in that very place Eochaid was defeated, and he forfeited his stake.

'My stake is forfeit to thee,' said Eochaid.

'Had I wished it, it had been forfeit long ago,' said Mider.

'What is it that thou desirest me to grant?' said Eochaid.

'That I may hold Etain in my arms, and obtain a kiss from her!' answered Mider.

Eochaid was silent for a while, and then he said: 'One month from this day thou shalt come, and that very thing that thou hast asked for shall be given to thee.' Now for a year before that Mider first came to Eochaid for the chess-play, had he been at the wooing of Etain, and he obtained her not; and the name which he gave to Etain was Béfind, or Fair-haired Woman, so it was that he said:

Wilt thou come to my home, fair-haired lady?

as has before been recited. And it was at that time that Etain said: 'If thou obtainest me from him who is the master of my house, I will go; but if thou are not able to obtain me from him, then I will not go.' And thereon Mider came to Eochaid, and allowed him at the first to win the victory over him, in order that Eochaid should stand in his debt; and therefore it was that he paid the great stakes to which he had agreed; and therefore also was it that he had demanded of him that he should play that game in ignorance of what was staked. And when Mider and his folk were paying those agreed-on stakes, which were paid upon that night; to wit, the making of the road, and the clearing of the stones from Meath, the rushes from around Tethba, and of the forest that is over Breg, it was thus that he spoke, as it is written in the Book of Drom Snechta:

Pile on the soil; thrust on the soil:
Red are the oxen around who toil:
Heavy the troops that my words obey;
Heavy they seem, and yet men are they.
Strongly, as piles, are the tree-trunks placed:
Red are the wattles above them laced:
Tired are your hands, and your glances slant;
One woman's winning this toil may grant!

Oxen ye are, but revenge shall see;
Men who are white shall your servants be:
Rushes from Teffa are cleared away:
Grief is the price that the man shall pay:
Stones have been cleared from the rough Meath ground;
Whose shall the gain or the harm be found?

Now Mider appointed a day at the end of the month when he was to meet Eochaid, and Eochaid called the armies of the heroes of Ireland together, so that they came to Tara; and all the best of the champions of Ireland, ring within ring, were about Tara, and they were in the midst of Tara itself, and they guarded it, both without and within; and the king and the queen were in the midst of the palace, and the outer court thereof was shut and locked, for they knew that the great might of men would come upon them. And upon the appointed night Etain was dispensing the banquet to the kings, for it was her duty to pour out the wine, when in the midst of their talk they saw Mider standing before them in the centre of the palace. He was always fair, yet fairer than he ever was seemed Mider to be upon that night. And he brought to amazement all the hosts on which he gazed, and all thereon were silent, and the king gave a welcome to him.

'Thy reception is such as I expected when I came,' said Mider; 'let that now be given to me that hath been promised. 'Tis a debt that is due when a promise hath been made; and I for my part have given to thee all that was promised by me.'

'I have not yet considered the matter,' said Eochaid.

'Thou hast promised Etain's very self to me,' said Mider; 'that is what hath come from thee.' Etain blushed for shame when she heard that word.

'Blush not,' said Mider to Etain, 'for in nowise hath thy wedding-feast been disgraced. I have been seeking thee for a year with the fairest jewels and treasures that can be found in Ireland, and I have not taken thee until the time came when Eochaid might permit it. 'Tis not through any will of thine that I have won thee.' 'I myself told thee,' said Etain, 'that until Eochaid should resign me to thee I would grant thee nothing. Take me then for my part, if Eochaid is willing to resign me to thee.'

'But I will not resign thee!' said Eochaid; 'nevertheless he shall take thee in his arms upon the floor of this house as thou art.'

'It shall be done!' said Mider.

He took his weapons into his left hand and the woman beneath his right shoulder; and he carried her off through the skylight of the house. And the hosts rose up around the king, for they felt that they had been disgraced, and they saw two swans circling round Tara, and the way that they took was the way to the elf-mound of Femun. And Eochaid with an army of the men of Ireland went to the elf-mound of Femun, which men call the mound of the Fair-haired-Women. And he followed the counsel of the men of Ireland, and he dug up each of the elf-mounds that he might take his wife from thence. And Mider and his host opposed them and the war between them was long: again and again the trenches made by Eochaid were destroyed, for nine years as some say lasted the strife of the men of Ireland to enter into the fairy palace. And when at last the armies of Eochaid came by digging to the borders of the fairy mansion, Mider sent to the side of the palace sixty women all in the shape of Etain, and so like to her that none could tell which was the queen. And Eochaid himself was deceived, and he chose, instead of Etain, her daughter Messbuachalla (or as some say Esa.) But when he found that he had been deceived, he returned again to sack Bri Leith, and this time Etain made herself known to Eochaid, by proofs that he could not mistake, and he bore her away in triumph to Tara, and there she abode with the king.

The Pursuit of Diarmaid and Gráinne

*This is a slightly condensed version of another of the great
romantic tales of Ireland, 'Tóraíocht Dhiarmada agus
Ghráinne'. The translation is that prepared by Neasa Ní Shé
in 1967. The story begins with the early rising one morning of
Fionn mac Cumhaill at Allen in Leinster.
On being questioned by his son, Oisín, why he had
awakened so early, Fionn replied:*

'Not without cause have I made this early rising, Oisín, for
I am a year without a wife and without a spouse since
Maghnais daughter of Garaidh Glúndubh mac Morna
died, for he is not wont to have slumber or comfort who is without a
fitting wife. And that is the cause of this early rising, Oisín.'

The story then goes on:

'What causes you to be thus?' said Oisín, 'for there is neither wife nor
spouse in green-meadowed islanded Ireland upon whom a man of
your worth would fix the keenness of his eye or of his sight that he
would not secure her; and further, there is not a daughter of a king or
a noble lord in the far regions of the great world upon whom you,
Fionn, would fix the keenness of your eye or of your sight, that we
ourselves would not bring her, freely or by force, to you.'

Then Diorraing spoke and he said:

'I know a fitting wife and spouse for you, Fionn, if you would care
to go and seek her.'

'Who is she?' said Fionn.

'Gráinne, daughter of Cormac son of Art son of Conn the
Hundred-battler,' said Diorraing, 'that is, the woman of the finest
shape and form and speech of the women of the whole world.'

31

*Once the suggestion had been made that Gráinne, daughter of
King Cormac of Tara, might be a suitable bride for Fionn, an
assembly was arranged at Tara so that the arrangements for the
betrothal might be made. Gráinne, however, was by no means
happy at the prospect of being wed to the elderly Fionn, and,
having caused a drug to be administered to the others present,
she embarked on a little plan of her own.*

The maid brought the goblet to Cairbre and he drank a draught out
of it, and he was scarcely able to give it to the person nearest to him
when he himself fell into a deep slumber and sound sleep, and each
one that would take the goblet, one after another, would fall into the
same state. And when Gráinne found everyone in a state of drunken-
ness and confusion she herself rose quietly and steadily from where
she was sitting and sat between Oisín son of Fionn and Diarmaid ó
Duibhne, and she spoke to Oisín and this is what she said:

'I wonder at Fionn mac Cumhaill,' said she, 'that he should ask
such a wife as I, for it would be more proper to give me such as you
than a man who is older than myself.'

'Do not say that, Gráinne,' said Oisín, 'for if Fionn should hear
you saying that he would not have anything to do with you, and neither would I dare to have anything to do with you.'

'Will you accept courtship from me, Oisín?' said Gráinne.

'I will not,' said Oisín, 'for whatsoever woman is betrothed to
Fionn I would not have anything to do with her.'

Gráinne turned her face to Diarmaid ó Duibhne and this is what
she said:

'Will you accept courtship from me, son of Ó Duibhne,' said she,
'since Oisín will not accept it from me?'

'I will not,' said Diarmaid, 'for whatsoever woman is betrothed to
Oisín it is not right for me to have anything to do with her even were
she not betrothed to Fionn.'

'Then,' said Gráinne, 'I put you under bonds of strife and destruction, Diarmaid, that is, the pain of a woman in childbirth and the
vision of a dead man over water and the life of Niall Caille to reproach
you, if you do not take me with you out of this house to-night before
Fionn and the king of Ireland rise out of that sleep in which they are.'

'Wicked are those bonds which you have put on me, woman,' said Diarmaid, 'and why have you put those bonds on me rather than on all the sons of kings and noble lords in the Teach Miodhchuarta to-night, since there is not of all those one less worthy of a woman than me?'

'By your hand, son of Ó Duibhne,' said Gráinne, 'it is not without reason that I have put those bonds on you. One day when the king of Ireland was holding an assembly and a gathering upon the lawn of Tara, and Fionn and the seven battalions of the standing army of the Fiana happened to be there that day, a game of hurling began between Cairbre Lifeachair son of Cormac and Mac Lughach. The Fiana of Ireland rose on the side of Mac Lughach, and the men of Breagha and Meath and Cearmna and the Pillars of Tara rose on the side of Cairbre, and there was no one sitting in the assembly that day but the king of Ireland and Fionn and yourself, Diarmaid. And it happened that the game was going against Mac Lughach and you yourself rose up and took his hurley stick from the man nearest to you and you threw him to the ground and to the earth, and you won the goal three times that day against Cairbre and against the warriors of Tara. And I was in my own sunny chamber that day watching you, and I fixed the keenness of my eye and of my sight upon you that day, and I did not give that love to any other person from that time to this.'

'It is a wonder that you should give that love to me', said Diarmaid, 'instead of to Fionn since there is not in Ireland a man more worthy of a woman than he. And do you know, Gráinne,' said Diarmaid, 'on the night that Fionn is in Tara that it is he himself who has the keys of Tara, so that we cannot leave this place on that account?'

'That is not true,' said Gráinne, 'there is an escape-door out of my sunny chamber and we will go out through it.'

'It is a tabu of mine to go through any escape-door whatsoever.'

'Well then,' said Gráinne, 'I hear that every hero and battle-champion can go by the shafts of his javelins and by the staves of his spears in or out over the palisade of every fort and of every fine stead, and I will go by the escape-door and you follow me like that.'

Bound totally by the obligation that Gráinne had laid upon him, Diarmaid was compelled to follow her. They fled as far away from Tara as they could, pursued eventually by Fionn. Diarmaid, by recourse to various magic—and highly athletic—feats, succeeded in getting the better of a host sent by Fionn to trap them, and in this was assisted by Aonghas, his foster-father and also the God of Love. The story continues:

Aonghus rose early and said to Diarmaid:

'I will depart, son of Ó Duibhne,' said he, 'and I leave this advice with you, not to go into a tree of one trunk in fleeing from Fionn, and not to go into an underground cave which has only one entrance, and not to go into an island of the sea which has only one way leading to it,' and he said, 'whatever place you shall cook your meal do not eat it there, and whatever place you shall eat do not lie there, and whatever place you shall lie do not rise there.'

And he took leave and farewell of them at that place. After that Diarmaid and Gráinne went on due westward with the Shannon on their right hand, and to Críoch Fear Morc which is called Íbh Conaill Ghabhra now, and to broad, great and pleasant Sliabh Luachra, and on westward until they reached Gearr-abha na bhFian which is called Leamhain now; and Diarmaid killed a salmon on the bank of the Leamhain and he put it on spits, and he crossed the stream to eat it and he crossed the stream eastward to sleep.

Diarmaid and Gráinne rose early on the morrow and they went on directly westward until they came to Bogach Finnleithid, and they met a young warrior on the Bogach, and the shape and form of the young warrior were good except that he had not fitting weapons nor clothes. Diarmaid greeted him and he asked tidings of him.

'I am a young warrior seeking a lord,' said he. 'Muadhán is my name.'

'What will you do for me, young warrior?' said Diarmaid.

'I will do service in the day and watching at night for you,' said Muadhán.

'I am telling you,' said Gráinne, 'to retain the young warrior, for you will not always be without followers.'

They made bonds of contract and agreement with each other, and they went on westward until they came to Cárrthach, and when they reached the stream Muadhán asked them both to go on his back over across the stream.

'Both of us together would be a heavy burden for you,' said Gráinne.

He put Diarmaid and Gráinne on his back and both together went on his back over across the stream. And they went on westward until they came to the Beith, and when they reached the stream Muadhán did the same thing with them, and they went into an underground cave at the side of Currach Cinn Amuide over Tonn Tóime, and Muadhán made a bed of soft rushes and birch-tops under Diarmaid and Gráinne at the back of the cave, and he himself went into the wood nearest to him and he put a holly berry on the point of the hook and he went above the sea and he took a fish with that cast. And he put up the second berry and he killed the second fish, and he put up the third berry and he caught a third fish. And he put his hook and his fishing-line in his girdle and the rod beside the hole and he brought his three fish with him to where Diarmaid and Gráinne were. And he put the fish on spits and when it was cooked Muadhán said:

'I would give the dividing of this fish to you, Diarmaid,' said he.

'I would prefer you to divide it,' said Diarmaid.

'Then, Gráinne,' said Muadhán, 'I would give the dividing of it to you.'

'It suffices me that you divide it,' said Gráinne.

'Then if it were you that divided this fish, Diarmaid, you would have given the largest portion to Gráinne, and let you have the biggest fish here, Gráinne. And had it been Gráinne who divided it, it is to you, Diarmaid, she would have given the largest portion, and let you have the second biggest fish here, and I will have this smallest fish.'

Let it be known to you, reader, that Diarmaid still kept himself from sinning or uniting with Gráinne, and that he left a spit of cooked flesh without a bite taken out of it in Doire Dhá Bhaoth as a sign for Fionn and for the Fiana of Ireland that he had not sinned with Gráinne, and also, that he left the second time a salmon on the bank of the Leamhain cooked likewise. Wherefore it was that Fionn hastened after him. But we will discourse on that same subject again.

They ate their meal that night and Diarmaid and Gráinne went to the back of the cave to sleep, and Muadhán went in front of the cave to keep watch and guard for them until the day rose with its full light on the morrow. And Diarmaid rose early and he woke Gráinne and he told her to keep watch for Muadhán and that he himself would go to walk the country around him.

Diarmaid went on and he climbed to the summit of the mound that was nearest to him and he was observing the four points of the compass around him, that is eastward and westward, southward and northward. And he was not long there when he saw in the direction directly to the west a swift spirited fleet and a full and great company of ships coming towards the land. And the course that the people of the fleet took was to land at the foot of the hill west of the cave where Gráinne was. And nine times nine of the chieftains of the fleet came ashore, and Diarmaid went to ask tidings of them, and he greeted them and asked news of them who they were or of what country they were.

'We are three warrior-leaders of Muir nIocht,' said they, 'and Fionn mac Cumhaill sent word to us to seek us, that is, because of a forest marauder and brigand who is outlawed by him, namely Diarmaid ó Duibhne, and it is to curb him we have come now,' said they. 'And we have three venomous hounds and we will loose them on his track when we get tidings of him; and fire does not burn them and water does not drown them and weapons do not wound them; and we ourselves number ten hundred able men and each man of them is capable of fighting a hundred men.'

Diarmaid again succeeded in overcoming not only the three venomous hounds but the three warrior-leaders as well. Muadhán had to leave them, and it was at this stage in their elopement that Gráinne was able to fulfil the essential part of her plan.

And Diarmaid and Gráinne were sad and mournful after Muadhán and for want of the company of the gentle companionship with them.

After that, however, Diarmaid and Gráinne journeyed directly northward by the side of Sliabh Eachtghe and from that to the cantred of Ó Fiachrach until they reached Dubhros Ó bhFiachrach.

Gráinne was getting tired, and when she realised that she had no man to carry her except Diarmaid, since Muadhán parted from her, she gained courage and a lively spirit and she began to walk boldly by Diarmaid's side until an errant little splash of water sprang up beside her leg, so she said:

'Diarmaid,' said she, 'though your valour and your bravery be great in conflicts and in battle-places I think myself that that little drop of errant water is more daring than you are.'

'That is true, Gráinne,' said Diarmaid, 'though I have been for a long time keeping myself from you through fear of Fionn I will not suffer myself to be reproached by you any longer; and it is hard to trust women,' he said. And it was then for the first time that Diarmaid ó Duibhne of the bright-tooth made a wife of Gráinne, daughter of the king of Ireland. And when they came into the wood Diarmaid made a hunting booth for cooking right in the middle of the wood, and he killed a wild deer that night and they consumed their fill of meat and pure water. And Diarmaid rose early on the morrow and went to the Searbhán Lochlannach and made a bond of contract and agreement with him and got permission to hunt and to chase from him and never to touch his berries.

*The pursuit by Fionn continued relentlessly, and again Aonghas
came to Diarmaid's assistance. When Diarmaid and Gráinne
were up a tree, completely surrounded by Fionn's forces,
Aonghas decided to spirit Gráinne away.*

As regards Fionn, he sent the nine Garbhs of the Fiana to fall by Diarmaid ó Duibhne, namely, Garbh of Sliabh gCua and Garbh of Sliabh Crot and Garbh of Sliabh Cláire and Garbh of Sliabh Muice and Garbh of Áth Mór and Garbh of Áth Luain and Garbh of Áth Fraoich and Garbh of Sliabh Mis and Garbh of Druim Mór. And when the nine Garbhs fell Aonghus said that he would take Gráinne with him to the Brugh over the Boyne, and Diarmaid said that if he were alive he would follow them, and if Fionn should kill him whatever children Gráinne would have to rear them well and to send Gráinne to her father to Tara.

Aonghus took leave and farewell of Diarmaid then and neither Fionn nor the Fiana of Ireland saw them. It was then Diarmaid ó

Duibhne said in a high, clear and pure voice that he himself would go down to Fionn and the Fiana.

'If you had been willing to do that,' said Fionn, 'long ago you and I would have been reconciled.'

'It is not to make peace with you that I am going there,' said Diarmaid, 'but I do not want to leave this place without your knowing it.'

When Fionn heard that he put the seven battalions of the standing army of the Fiana round about the quicken tree and they put their shield straps together so that Diarmaid would not escape through them. When Diarmaid saw their hands in each others' hands round the quicken tree he put the shafts of his javelins under him and he rose out very lightly over everyone, and announced to Fionn and to the Fiana of Ireland that he had passed them, and he put his shield on the arched slope of his back, and the seven battalions of the standing army of the Fiana went after Diarmaid and they aimed together at him and not one of them did any harm to him until he went a long distance from them, and he turned back until he went on the track of Gráinne and Aonghus to the Brugh over the Boyne that night. And Gráinne and Aonghus were joyous at seeing Diarmaid and they consumed feasts and banquets that night until the following morning came.

And Aonghus rose early that day and he went to meet Fionn and the Fiana and he asked Fionn whether he would make peace with Diarmaid ó Duibhne. Fionn said there is no form whatever in which Diarmaid would ask peace that he himself would not grant it to him. It was then Aonghus went to Cormac mac Airt to seek peace for Diarmaid ó Duibhne from him, and Cormac said that he would grant him peace. And Aonghus went to Diarmaid and asked him whether he would make peace with Cormac and with Fionn. Diarmaid said he would make peace if he got the conditions which he would ask of them.

'What condition is that?' said Aonghus.

'The cantred of Corca Dhuibhne which my father had, that Fionn shall neither hunt nor chase there and without rent or tribute to the king of Ireland therefrom, and the cantred of Beann Damhuis Dubh-chairrge in Leinster as a gift for myself from Fionn, because it is the best cantred in Ireland, and the cantred of Céis Chorainn from the king of Ireland as dowry with his daughter for me. And those are the conditions upon which I would make peace with the king of Ireland and with Fionn,' said Diarmaid.

'Will you be at peace with those conditions if you get them?' said Aonghus.

'It would be easier for me to make peace by getting those conditions,' said Diarmaid.

It was then Aonghus went with those tidings to the king of Ireland and he went to Fionn, and he got all the conditions from them, and they forgave him all he had done to them while he had been outlawed. And Aonghus made peace between them for sixteen years. And the place that Diarmaid and Gráinne chose as a place and site for living was Ráith Ghráinne in the cantred of Céis Chorainn because of its distance from Fionn and from the king of Ireland. And Gráinne bore Diarmaid four sons and one daughter there, namely, Donnchadh and Eochaidh, Connla and Sealbhach Searcach and Druineach Dhil daughter of Diarmaid.

Eventually, of course, Fionn's jealousy overcame him, and by treachery he brought about poor Diarmaid's death.

Fionn and that company of the Fiana of Ireland went to leave the mound, with Mac an Chuill in Fionn's hand, and Oisín and Osgar and Caoilte and Mac Lughach returned and they put their four cloaks together on Diarmaid, and they themselves went on after Fionn and the Fiana, and no account is given of them until they reached Ráith Ghráinne. And Gráinne was before them out on the battlements of the rath waiting to get tidings of Diarmaid, and she saw Fionn and the Fiana of Ireland coming to her in that manner, and Gráinne said:

'If Diarmaid ó Duibhne were alive,' said she, 'it is not in Fionn's hand that Mac an Chuill would be coming to this place.'

And it is thus Gráinne was at that time, heavy and pregnant, and she fell out over the ramparts of the rath and gave birth to three dead sons on the spot. When Oisín saw the woman in travail he sent Fionn and the Fiana away from the place. As Fionn and the Fiana were leaving the place Gráinne lifted up her head and she asked Fionn to leave Mac an Chuill with herself. Fionn said he would not, and that he did not think it too much that he himself should have that much of Diarmaid ó Duibhne's inheritance. Oisín made for him and he took the hound from Fionn's hand and he brought it with him to Gráinne, and he himself followed his people.

Gráinne's household came out and they carried her with them into the rath. It was then Gráinne sent the three hundred of a household which she had to Beann Gulban for Diarmaid ó Duibhne's body to bring it to herself to Ráth Ghráinne. The household proceeded to Beann Gulban, and they found Aonghus of the Brugh there before them with his three hundred of a household around him over the body of Diarmaid ó Duibhne.

They entered Ráith Ghráinne together. And they were seated at the sides of the delightful hostel according to the nobility and the patrimony of each one, and they were served with mild tasty foods and moderate very sweet ales and strong fermented drinks in fair ornate drinking-horns until the chiefs became exhilarated and gently mirthful. It was then Gráinne daughter of Cormac spoke in a high, clear and pure voice in the midst of everyone and what she said was:

'Children of Diarmaid ó Duibhne,' said she, 'your father was killed by Fionn mac Cumhaill notwithstanding the agreements and conditions of their peace, and you avenge that well on him. And there are your portions of the inheritance of your father for you,' said she, 'namely, his weapons and his armour and his various sharp weapons. And I will myself divide them out among you, and I myself will have the goblets, the drinking-horns, the cups and the beautiful golden drinking vessels, and the kine and the cattle-herds undivided.'

And as she was saying that she recited the lay:

Arise, children of Diarmaid,
make your watchful attack:
may your adventure be successful,
the tidings of a good man have come to you.

This sword for Donnchadh,
the best son that Diarmaid had,
and the Ga Dearg for Eochaidh,
they lead to every advantage.

Give his breast-plate from me to Iollann,
safe every body on which it be put,
and the shield for Connla,
for the chief who upholds the battalions.

How Fionn Won His Bride

This little story takes us back to the youthful days of
Fionn mac Cumhaill and tells how, by a daring athletic feat,
he won the affections of the daughter of a king.
It is taken from the translation by Standish O'Grady in his
Finn and his Companions.

'After I escaped from the watery dún of that robber who had killed my friends and teachers, the six poets, I was with my two guardians once more in the Slieve Bloom forests. I used to hunt for them, and our larder was never empty. When I next went away, I came to Bantry, on the shore of the great bay of Bere in the south. I offered my services to the King of Bantry. He asked me what I could do, and I said I could hunt. The King of Bantry made me his hunter. I used to hunt for him in the woods and mountains of the wild countryside nearby. There was one spot there very dear to me on account of its beauty; it is called the Wild Glen (Glengariffe). There are beautiful little bays and inlets of the sea there, and mountains and streams, and delightful woods. The birds sing there in the winter. Once while I was hunting at a distance from home, I saw a crowd of people, kings and nobles, and noble ladies in holiday attire—a very gay and delightful scene. I came to the crowd and mixed with the wild people of the district who were onlookers. No one knew me in that place, nor was it known anywhere, except to my two guardians, that I was the lost son of Cumhall. Among the noble ladies was one seated on a throne, with others in attendance on her,

41

and guards. She was young, but looked proud. Never before in dreams or with my waking eyes had I seen any maiden so beautiful. I turned to a bystander and said: "Who is this princess who is like the morning star, and what is the meaning of this gathering?" She heard me, for there was a waiting silence upon the gathering, and turned her eyes towards me. Then she started, as I thought, and blushed, and looked away quickly.

'The bystander answered: "You are surely a stranger in this country. That princess, who is like the morning star for beauty, is the only daughter of the King of Ciarraí. Many noble youths and famous warriors have wanted her in marriage, but from the first she said that it was a *geas* to her (a druidic commandment) not to marry any man who could not leap yonder deep split in the mountain side; and truly it is an awful leap, and those who have attempted it are at the bottom of the split. This morning a king's son named Criomthann has promised to leap the split or die there like others."

'I pushed through the wild people, and knew that she was ever aware of my doings even when pride stopped her from looking towards me. I was clad in my skins, and these tied together any way. I came to the nobles, and bowing to them, asked whether I might pass through and look at the split. For answer, two of them tried to push me back, but I stood like a rock against them, and they and others at the same time raised against me their voices and their weapons. The maiden was alarmed at this, and said: "Let the hunter examine the split if it be pleasing to him. See you not that he is a stranger?" All in my skins as I was, truly a wild sight, I bowed low to the maiden, and thanked her for her kindness, and went to the edge. Far below, a torrent ran through the ravine, so distant that it was dumb; and at the other side were sharp stones and crooked points of rock. I measured the distance with my eye, and felt certain that I could make the leap, for, owing to my manner of life, I was truly a good leaper. I returned, and, because I had found favour in her eyes, came and took my stand among the nobles and men of war, and was well received by them this second time.

'Then from the west there came a splendid company, led by a young man nobly dressed, wearing a brooch of gold in his five-times-folded mantle; a very graceful youth, whose form and shapely limbs seemed to promise success in that venture, so that the blood seemed to stand still in my heart for fear that he might succeed, and when I looked to the maid she was pale, too, fearing that the young man might make the leap.

'He came near, and having made her a bow, and addressed her and her people, he withdrew, and stripped off his mantle and jerkin of fine satin, so that there was upon him only a close-fitting light shirt. He took off his shoes, too, and put on others carefully prepared for such a deed. Then, when he was ready, a trumpet sounded, and he ran towards the chasm as swiftly as a deer, so that I said: "Surely the man will leap the split and I shall die." But when he neared the chasm and saw the crooked rocks and stones at the other side, and saw the dark, fearsome depths of the ravine, he hesitated and swerved, not taking the leap. Then the maiden looked at me, and from her two eyes, and her lips, and her whole face, I saw love for myself pour forth in torrents, and she saw the same flow from me to her.

'The young man, Criomthann, when he had been encouraged by his people, tried the leap a second time, and yet a third, but he ever swerved, not making the leap; and in the end broke into tears and went away. Then I arose, and, taking courage, stood before the throne and offered to take the leap which Criomthann had refused, if the maid would accept me for her husband. She was silent and pale with terror, and did not answer. Her father and the nobles told me that she would not, and, laughing, they said to save my neck for the service of my king, and that whole bones were better than broken ones.

'I said that I would not take an answer from them, only from the damsel, that it was her and not any of them I wished to marry. She said something in a low voice to her father. He raised his head and said, laughing:

'"She says that she never saw anyone worse dressed."

'"That may be," I answered, "but it is not my skins that I offer as a husband, but myself, and my question is not answered."

'After a further talk, her father spoke again:

'"My daughter is sorry to have sneered at your clothes, and she could wish her husband in other things to be like you, but will not agree to the leap."

'"Then," said I, "if the damsel will not give me the same promise that she made to others, I shall leap the split, and having reached the far side I shall return to my lord."

'When she heard that, and saw that I had my mind made up, she burst into tears and agreed, and her father said:

'"I am truly sorry for you, O brave youth, and how shall I make an excuse to your lord, who is my foster-brother, when he learns that we have killed his man?"

'Then rejoicing, I chose my distance from the edge, and I threw off none of my attire, only laced it with a thong close to me that the skins might not hinder me in my flight over the cleft. And I ran to the edge and sprang, though a woman's scream rang in my ears, and rose like a bird, and landed with my two feet on the other side on smooth ground beyond the rocks, and in like manner I sprang back, and I asked them whether that was enough, speaking slowly, for I was in no way out of breath. They were astonished and pale, but when I offered to do it again they said that it was enough.

'In this way I won my dear wife.

'I went with that company to the King of Ciarraí's palace, and I got there splendid clothes fit for a king's son, and we were married with great honour. And now, dear friends, I tell you one of my secrets. My wife can foresee things. It was revealed to her that my death would come swift and bloody in any year in which I might neglect to take that leap both backwards and forwards on the first day of May, from the East to the West at the rising of the sun, and from the West to the East at his setting.'

When Fionn lay down and slept that night the old men talked with each other joyfully in low voices, but indeed that was not necessary, for Fionn's sleep could not be disturbed or broken by the voices of friends.

The Book of the Lays of Fionn

*These two poems are inserted here, despite their being dated to
the thirteenth or fourteenth century, because of their
connection with the legends of Fionn. The first is a very moving
conversation between Goll mac Morna and his wife before
his death; the translation is by Eoin Mac Néill. The second is a
little allegorical poem, translated by Gerard Murphy.
Both poets are, regrettably, anonymous.*

'Woman, take away my tunic: rise up and go from me:
prepare to depart, clear one of rosy cheeks, the morn
before my slaying.'

'O Goll, what way shall I take? alas for those whose friends are
few! rare is the woman that has grace, when she is left without head,
without lord.'

'Seek the camp of Fionn of the Fiana in its place on this westward side; wed there, gentle one of red lips, some good man worthy
of thee.'

'What man there might I wed, my great Goll that wast kind to
me? where might I find west or east thy equal for a bed-fellow?'

'Wilt thou have Oisin son of Fionn, or Aonghus son of Aodh
Rinn, or muscular bloodstained Caireall, or the hundred-wounding
Corr Chos-luath?'

'Conall of Cruachain is my father: I am fellow-fosterling to Conn
of the Hundred Battles: brother to me in the northern land is
Ceidghein son of shaft-stout Conall.

'It is the harder for me to leave thee, that thou art my gentle
sweet first husband: seven years of bravery agone, thou broughtest
me, husband, to thy couch.

'From that night until to-night, thou hast not shown me a harsh

45

mind: from this night out I will not be light-minded, I will belong to no man on the surface of earth.

'Thirty days living without food scarcely was ever man before thee: a hundred heroes, Goll, by thy hand have fallen on the narrow crag.'

'Wide is the sea around us, and I on the narrow of the crag: hunger for food is betraying me, and thirst is overmatching me.

'Though hunger for food is betraying me, though fierce is the warfare of the five battalions, still more it takes the beauty from my cheek, to have to drink bitter-strong brine.

'My own twenty-nine brothers if one man of the Fian had killed, it would make my peace with him were he to relieve me for one night from thirst.'

'Goll son of Morna from Magh Maoin, eat those bodies at thy side: it will relieve thy thirst after eating of the men to drink the milk of my breasts.'

'Daughter of Conall, I will not hide it—ah! it is pitiful how this thing has befallen—woman's bidding north or south I will not do and have never done.'

'Ah! Goll, it is a woeful plight, five battalions or six against thee, and thou on the corner of a hard crag, a bare lofty chilly crag.'

'That, O red mouth that wast musical, was my one fear on wave or land—Fionn and his Fian pressing on me and I without food in a narrow corner.

'I have stained my shafts right well in the bodies of the House of Tréanmhór: I have inflicted on them suffering and hardship, I have killed shaft-strong Cumhall.

'I brought the Munstermen to grief on the Tuesday in Magh Léana: I delivered battle bravely on the morn in Magh Eanaigh.

'Eochaidh Red-spot son of Mál, of Ulster's proud-faced over-king, I plunged into that hero my spear: I brought them to sorrow, woman.'

. . . .

These six: three to whom I come going righthandwise, three who are vehement treacherous and crooked and three who are slender of body and white of skin.

Trouble: she is the woman who has come to me; manifest is the trace of her two feet; where she treads she treads not lightly.

Lovemaking: she who beguiles every company; though she be dearer than life I have no memory of her.

Mildness: happy the person to whom she is companion; preference has never gone from her to another; she is better than the choicest dowry.

Necessity: a surly wretch from the day of the first man, stronger than all women; to control her is impossible.

High spirit: a noble courteous and excellent queen; though the woman herself be dear, since last year she has not come to me.

Grief: she wears black garments; I welcome not a woman so diligent: her tidings are not least.

The Lament of Créidhe, Daughter of Guaire of Aidhne

Créidhe, daughter of Guaire, sang these quatrains for Díneartach, son of Guaire, son of Neachtan. She had seen him in the battle of Aidhne, wherein he had received seventeen woundings on the breast of his tunic. She loved him after that. The translation is by Gerard Murphy.

The arrows that murder sleep, at every hour in the cold night, are love-lamenting, by reason of times spent, after day, in the company of one from beside the land of Roigne.

Great love for a man of another land who excelled his coevals has taken my bloom; it allows me no sleep.

Sweeter than all songs was his speech save holy adoration of Heaven's King: glorious flame without a word of boasting, slender softsided mate.

When I was a child I was modest: I used not to be engaged on the evil business of lust; since I reached the uncertainty of age my wantonness has begun to beguile me.

I have everything good with Gúaire, the king of cold Aidne; but my mind seeks to go from my people to the land which is in Irlúachair.

In the land of glorious Aidne, around the sides of Cell Cholmáin, men sing of a glorious flame, from the south of Limerick of the graves, whose name is Dínertach.

His grievous death, holy Christ, torments my kindly heart: these are the arrows that murder sleep at every hour in the cold night.

Liain and Cuirithir

Liain (to whom this poem is sometimes attributed) and Cuirithir were victims of a sort of Héloïse and Abélard situation: both were poets and in love; she, however, became a nun. In this poem, translated by Gerard Murphy, she expresses her regret for her action.

Unpleasing is that deed which I have done: what I loved I have vexed.

Were it not for fear of the King of Heaven, it had been madness for one who would not do what Cuirithir wished.

Not profitless to him was that which he desired, to reach Heaven and avoid pain.

A trifle vexed Cuirithir in regard to me; my gentleness towards him was great.

I am Líadan; I loved Cuirithir; this is as true as anything told.

For a short time I was in the company of Cuirithir; to be with me was profitable to him.

Forest music used to sing to me beside Cuirithir, together with the sound of the fierce sea.

I should have thought that no arrangement I might make would have vexed Cuirithir in regard to me.

Conceal it not: he was my heart's love, even though I should love all others besides.

A roar of fire has split my heart; without him for certain it will not live.

A Dead Wife

This poem by Muiríoch Albanach Ó Dálaigh, a lament for a dead wife, is particularly poignant. It dates from the thirteenth century; a unique copy exists in the Book of the Dean of Lismore. It has been edited and translated by Osborn Bergin; the translation here was given as a working translation to her students by my first wife, Deirdre Flanagan, shortly before her own death in 1984. The entire Early Modern Irish text is given as well.

M'anam do sgar riomsa a-raoir:
    calann ghlan dob ionnsa i n-uaigh;
rugadh bruinne maordha mín
    is aonbhla lí uime uainn.

Do tógbhadh sgath aobhdha fhionn
    a-mach ar an bhfaongha bhfann:
laogh mo chridhise do chrom,
    craobh throm an tighise thall.

M'aonar a-nocht damhsa, a Dhé,
    olc an saoghal camsa ad-chí;
dob álainn trom an taoibh naoi
    do bhaoi sonn a-raoir, a Rí.

Truagh leam an leabasa thiar,
    mo pheall seadasa dhá snámh;
tárramair corp seada saor
    is folt claon, a leaba, id lár.

Do bhí duine go ndreich moill
    ina luighe ar leith mo phill;
gan bharamhail acht bláth cuill
    don sgáth duinn bhanamhail bhinn.

Maol Mheadha na malach ndonn
    mo dhabhach mheadha a-raon rom;
mo chridhe an sgáth do sgar riom,
    bláth mhionn arna car do chrom.

Táinig an chlí as ar gcuing,
    agus dí ráinig mar roinn:
corp idir dá aisil inn
    ar dtocht don fhinn mhaisigh mhoill.

Leath mo throigheadh, leath mo thaobh,
    a dreach mar an droighean bán,
níor dhísle neach dhí ná dhún,
    leath mo shúl í, leath mo lamh.

Leath mo chuirp an choinneal naoi;
    's guirt riom do rionneadh, a Rí;
agá labhra is meirtneach mé—
    dob é ceirleath m'anma í.

Mo chéadghrádh a dearc mhall mhór,
    déadbhán agus cam a cliabh:
nochar bhean a colann caomh
    ná a taobh ré fear romham riamh.

Fiche bliadhna inne ar-aon,
    fá binne gach bliadhna ar nglór,
go rug éinleanabh déag dhún,
    an ghéag úr mhéirleabhar mhór.

Gé tú, nocha n-oilim ann,
  ó do thoirinn ar gcnú chorr;
ar sgaradh dár roghrádh rom,
  falamh lom an domhnán donn.

Ón ló do sáidheadh cleath corr
  im theach nochar ráidheadh rum—
ní thug aoighe d'ortha ann
  dá barr naoidhe dhorcha dhunn.

A dhaoine, ná coisgidh damh;
  faoiche ré cloistin ní col;
táinig luinnchreach lom 'nar dteagh—
  an bhruithneach gheal donn ar ndol.

Is é rug uan í 'na ghrúg,
  Rí na sluagh is Rí na ród;
beag an cion do chúl na ngéag
  a héag ó a fior go húr óg.

Ionmhain lámh bhog do bhí sonn,
  a Rí na gclog is na gceall:
ach! an lámh nachar logh mionn,
  crádh liom gan a cor fám cheann.

• • • • • • • • • • • • • • • •

My soul parted from me last night
The pure beloved body is in the grave now
The smooth proud breast was taken from me
Wrapped in a linen sheet

A fair beautiful flower
has been plucked from the delicate bent stalk
The darling of my heart has drooped
Laden branch of yonder house

Alone am I tonight Oh God
Wretched is this torturous world you see
Lovely was the weight of the young body
That was here last night

Sad for me is yonder bed
My own long pallet a-swim in it
We have seen in you oh! bed a long
noble form with waving hair

A person of gentle aspect
lay alongside my pallet
The flower of the hazel alone
Could compare to the dark shadow womanly sweet-voiced

Maol Mheadha of the brown eyebrows
My vessel of mead alongside me
My heart the shadow that has parted from me
Flower of jewels after being planted has wilted

My body has gone from my control
And has fallen to her share
A body in two parts am I
Since the fair beautiful gentle one has gone

One of my feet, one of my sides
Her countenance like the whitethorn
No one belonged more to her than to me
She was one of my eyes, one of my hands

She was one half of my body, the bright candle flame
Harshly have I been dealt with oh! King:
To speak of it leaves me weak
She was the very half of my soul

Her large gentle eye was my first love
Ivory white and curved her breasts
Her fair body and person
Who belonged to no man before me

Twenty years were we together
Our voices more in accord every year
She bore me eleven children
The tall fresh long-fingered branch

Though I live, I do not nourish in it
I am no more
Since my poor hazelnut has fallen
Since my great love has parted from me
Dark and empty is the vain dark world

Since the day when a smooth wattle
Was fixed in my house it has not been said to me
No guest has put a spell within
On her fresh dusky brown hair

Oh people do not restrain me
There is no ban on weeping
A bare merciless pillage has been done on my house
The fair brown-haired glowing one has gone

It was he who snatched her from us in his displeasure
King of the roads
Little was it the fault of the curly-haired one
To die and leave her husband while fresh and young

Dear is the soft hand that was here
Oh! King of bells and of churchyards
Alas! the hand that never swore an oath
It tortures me that it is not placed under my head

The Midnight Court

*This lengthy poem by Brian Merriman, 'Cúirt an Mheán
Oíche', is conceived as a sort of judicial inquiry or
court case between men and women to determine why men were
loath to marry. In turn the women and the men state their cases.
Given below are the first statement on behalf of the women,
taken from a verse translation by Percy Ussher published in
1926 with a foreword by W. B. Yeats, and the reply on behalf of
the men from a translation by Frank O'Connor.*

Weary of woe, with sorrow sated,
She dried her eyes, her sighs surmounted,
And in these words her woes recounted:—
'We give you greeting, Eevell fair,
Gracious queen, your people's care,
Who pity the poor and relieve their plight
And save the brave and retrieve the right.
'Tis the cause of my anguish and grief of heart,
The source of my sorrow and inward smart,
My wounding rending pain unending,
The way our women thro' life are wending,
Gray, gloomy nuns with the grave pursuing,
Since our men and maidens have left off wooing;
Myself among them condemned to wait
Without hope and mope in the maiden state,
Without husband heaping the golden store
Or children creeping on hearth and floor,
In dread and fear—a drear subsistence—
Of finding nought to support existence,
By troubles pressed and by rest forsaken,
By cares consumed and by sorrows shaken.
Chaste Eevell, hasten to the relief

Of the women of Erin in their grief,
Wasting their pains in vain endeavour
To meet with mates who elude them ever,
Till in the ages is such disparity
We would not touch them except from charity,
With bleary eyes and wry grimaces
To scare a maiden from their embraces.
And if in manhood's warm pulsation
A youth is tempted to change his station,
He chooses a dour and sour-faced scold
Who's wasted her days in raising gold;
No lively lass of sweet seventeen
Of figure neat and features clean,
But blear-eyed hag or harridan brown
With toothless jaws and hairless crown
And snotty nose and dun complexion
And offering constant shrill correction.
My heart is torn and worn with grieving,
And my breast distressed with restless heaving,
With torture dull and with desperation
At the thought of my dismal situation,
When I see a bonny and bold young blade
With comely features and frame displayed,
A sturdy swearer or spanking buck,
A sprightly strapper with spunk and pluck,
A goodly wopper well made and planned,
A gamey walloper gay and grand,
Nimble and brave and bland and blithe,
Eager and active and brisk and lithe,
Of noted parts and of proved precocity,
Sold to a scold or old hideosity,
Withered and worn and blear and brown,
A mumbling, grumbling, garrulous clown,
A surly, sluttish and graceless gawk
Knotted and gnarled like a cabbage's stalk,
A sleepy, sluggish decayed old stump,
A useless, juiceless and faded frump.

Ah, woe is me! there's a crumpled crone
Being buckled to-night while I'm left lone,
She's a surly scold and a bold-faced jade
And this moment she's merry—and me a maid!
Why wouldn't they have myself in marriage?
I'm comely and shapely, of stately carriage,
I've a mouth and a smile to make men dream
And a forehead that's fair with ne'er a seam,
My teeth are pearls in a peerless row,
Cherries to vie with my lips pray show,
I've a dancing, glancing, entrancing eye,
Roguish and rakish and takish and sly,
Gold lacks lustre beside my hair,
And every curl might a saint ensnare,
My cheeks are smooth without stain or spot,
Dimpled and fresh without blemish or blot,
My throat, my hands, my neck, my face,
Rival each other in dainty grace,
I've hips and ankles and lips and breast
And limbs to offer as good as the best.
Look at my waist tight-laced and slim,
I'm not coarse or ragged or rank of limb,
Not stringy or scraggy or lanky or lean
But as fair a female as e'er was seen,
A pleasing, teasing and tempting tart
That might coax and entice the coldest heart.
If I were a tasteless, graceless baggage,
A slummocky scut of cumbrous carriage,
A sloven or slut or frump or fright,
Or maid morose and impolite,
An awkward gawk of ungainly make,
A stark and crooked and stiff old stake,
A senseless, sightless bent old crone,
I'm ever on view to the crowds that pass
At market or meeting or Sunday Mass,
At supper or social or raffle or race
Or wherever the gayest are going the pace,

At party or pattern or picnic or fete
In hopes that I'd click with some lad soon or late;
But all my pursuit is a futile endeavour,
They've baulked me and bilked me and slipped from me ever,
They've baffled my schemes and my best-conceived art,
They've spurned me and turned from me and tattered my heart;
After all my advances, my ogling and sighing,
My most killing glances, my coaxing and eyeing,
After all I have spent upon readers of palms
And tellers of tea-leaves and sellers of charms.
There isn't a plan you can conceive
For Christmas or Easter or All Saints' Eve,
At the moon's eclipse or the New Year's chime
That I haven't attempted time on time.
I never would sleep a night in bed
Without fruit-stuffed stocking beneath my head,
I wouldn't complain if they left me alone.
I've never been present that I'm aware
At wedding or wake or fete or fair,
At the racing-ring or the hurling-ground
Or wherever the menfolk may be found,
But I've managed to make some shape and show
And been bedizened from top to toe
With stylish hood and starched coiffure
And powder-sprinkled chevelure,
My speckled gown with ribbons tied
And ruffles with the richest vied,
With cardinal of scarlet hue
And facings pleasing to the view,
And cambric apron gaily sown
With blowsy flowers of kind unknown,
And rigid hoops and buckled shoes
With smooth high heels attached by screws
And silken gloves and costly lace
And flounces, fringes, frills and stays.
Mind, do not think I'm an artless gull,
A stupid, unsocial or bashful trull,

Timid, a prey to wayward fancies,
Or shy or ashamed of a man's advances …'

'Your worship, 'tis women's sinful pride
And that alone has the world destroyed.
Every young man that's ripe for marriage
Is hooked like this by some tricky baggage,
And no one is secure, for a friend of my own,
As nice a boy as ever I've known
That lives from me only a perch or two—
God help him!—married misfortune too.
It breaks my heart when she passes by
With her saucy looks and head held high,
Cows to pasture and fields of wheat,
And money to spare—and all deceit!
Well-fitted to rear a tinker's clan,
She waggles her hips at every man,
With her brazen face and bullock's hide,
And such airs and graces, and mad with pride.
And—that God may judge me!—only I hate
A scandalous tongue, I could relate
Things of that woman's previous state
As one with whom every man could mate
In any convenient field or gate
As the chance might come to him early or late!
But now, of course, we must all forget
Her galloping days and the pace she set;
The race she ran in Ibrackane,
In Manishmore and Teermaclane,
With young and old of the meanest rabble
Of Ennis, Clareabbey and Quin astraddle!
Toughs from Tradree out on a fling,
And Cratlee cut-throats sure to swing;
But still I'd say 'twas the neighbours' spite,
And the girl did nothing but what was right,
But the devil take her and all she showed!
I found her myself on the public road,

On the naked earth with a bare backside
And a Garus turf-cutter astride!
Is it any wonder my heart is failing,
That I feel that the end of the world is nearing,
When, ploughed and sown to all men's knowledge,
She can manage the child to arrive with marriage,
And even then, put to the pinch,
Begrudges Charity an inch;
For, counting from the final prayer
With the candles quenched and the altar bare
To the day when her offspring takes the air
Is a full nine months with a week to spare?

'But you see the troubles a man takes on!
From the minute he marries his peace is gone;
Forever in fear of a neighbour's sneer—
And my own experience cost me dear.
I lived alone as happy as Larry
Till I took it into my head to marry,
Tilling my fields with an easy mind,
Going wherever I felt inclined,
Welcomed by all as a man of price,
Always ready with good advice.
The neighbours listened—they couldn't refuse
For I'd money and stock to uphold my views—
Everything came at my beck and call
Till a woman appeared and destroyed it all:
A beautiful girl with ripening bosom,
Cheeks as bright as apple-blossom,
Hair that glimmered and foamed in the wind,
And a face that blazed with the light behind;
A tinkling laugh and a modest carriage
And a twinkling eye that was ripe for marriage.
I goggled and gaped like one born mindless
Till I took her face for a form of kindness,
Though that wasn't quite what the Lord intended
For He marked me down like a man offended

For a vengeance that wouldn't be easy mended
With my folly exposed and my comfort ended.

'Not to detain you here all day
I married the girl without more delay,
And took my share in the fun that followed.
There was plenty for all and nothing borrowed.
Be fair to me now! There was no one slighted;
The beggarmen took the road delighted;
The clerk and mummers were elated;
The priest went home with his pocket weighted.
The lamps were lit, the guests arrived;
The supper was ready, the drink was plied;
The fiddles were flayed, and, the night advancing,
The neighbours joined in the sport and dancing.

'A pity to God I didn't smother
When first I took the milk from my mother,
Or any day I ever broke bread
Before I brought that woman to bed!
For though everyone talked of her carouses
As a scratching post of the public houses
That as sure as ever the glasses would jingle
Flattened herself to married and single,
Admitting no modesty to mention,
I never believed but 'twas all invention.
They added, in view of the life she led,
I might take to the roads and beg my bread,
But I took it for talk and hardly minded—
Sure, a man like me could never be blinded!—
And I smiled and nodded and off I tripped
Till my wedding night when I saw her stripped,
And knew too late that this was no libel
Spread in the pub by some jealous rival—
By God, 'twas a fact, and well-supported:
I was a father before I started!

'So there I was in the cold daylight,
A family man after one short night!
The women around me, scolding, preaching,
The wife in bed and the baby screeching.
I stirred the milk as the kettle boiled
Making a bottle to give the child;
All the old hags at the hob were cooing
As if they believed it was all my doing—
Flattery worse than ever you heard:
"Glory and praise to our blessed Lord,
Though he came in a hurry, the poor little creature,
He's the spit of his da in every feature.
Sal, will you look at the cut of that lip!
There's fingers for you! Feel his grip!
Would you measure the legs and the rolls of fat!
Was there ever a seven-month child like that!"
And they traced away with great preciseness
My matchless face in the baby's likeness;
The same snub nose and frolicsome air,
And the way I laugh and the way I stare;
And they swore that never from head to toe
Was a child that resembled his father so.
But they wouldn't let me go near the wonder—
"Sure, a draught would blow the poor child asunder!"
All of them out to blind me further—
"The least little breath would be noonday murder!"
Malice and lies! So I took the floor,
Mad with rage and I cursed and swore,
And bade them all to leave my sight.
They shrank away with faces white,
And moaned as they handed me the baby:
"Don't crush him now! Can't you handle him easy?
The least thing hurts them. Treat him kindly!
Some fall she got brought it on untimely.
Don't lift his head but leave him lying!
Poor innocent scrap, and to think he's dying!
If he lives at all till the end of day
Till the priest can come 'tis the most we'll pray!"

'I off with the rags and set him free,
And studied him well as he lay on my knee.
That too, by God, was nothing but lies
For he staggered myself with his kicks and cries.
A pair of shoulders like my own,
Legs like sausages, hair fullgrown;
His ears stuck out and his nails were long,
His hands and wrists and elbows strong;
His eyes were bright, his nostrils wide,
And the knee-caps showing beneath his hide—
A champion, begod, a powerful whelp,
As healthy and hearty as myself!

'Young woman, I've made my case entire.
Justice is all that I require.
Once consider the terrible life
We lead from the minute we take a wife,
And you'll find and see that marriage must stop
And the men unmarried must be let off.
And, child of grace, don't think of the race;
Plenty will follow to take our place;
There are ways and means to make lovers agree
Without making a show of men like me.
There's no excuse for all the exploiters;
Cornerboys, clerks and priests and pipers—
Idle fellows that leave you broke
With the jars of malt and the beer they soak,
When the Mother of God herself could breed
Without asking the views of clerk or creed.
Healthy and happy, wholesome and sound,
The come-by-twilight sort abound;
No one assumes but their lungs are ample,
And their hearts as sound as the best example.
When did Nature display unkindness
To the bastard child in disease or blindness?
Are they not handsomer, better-bred
Than many that come of a lawful bed?

'I needn't go far to look for proof
For I've one of the sort beneath my roof—
Let him come here for all to view!
Look at him now! You see 'tis true.
Agreed, we don't know his father's name,
But his mother admires him just the same,
And if in all things else he shines
Who cares for his baptismal lines?
He isn't a dwarf or an old man's error,
A paralytic or walking terror,
He isn't a hunchback or a cripple
But a lightsome, laughing gay young divil.
'Tis easy to see he's no flash in the pan;
No sleepy, good-natured, respectable man,
Without sinew or bone or belly or bust,
Or venom or vice or love or lust,
Buckled and braced in every limb
Spouted the seed that flowered in him:
For back and leg and chest and height
Prove him to all in the teeth of spite
A child begotten in fear and wonder
In the blood's millrace and the body's thunder.'

Eibhlín, a Rún (Eileen Aroon)

*This is probably the best-known love song in Irish music.
It is said to have been written by the harper Cearbhall Ó
Dálaigh in the seventeenth century. According to tradition,
he was in love with Eibhlín Kavanagh, a daughter of
noble family. They did not approve of Ó Dálaigh as a suitor,
so another, more suitable marriage was arranged for her.*

*Cearbhall, however, appeared in disguise at the wedding and,
by singing this song, persuaded Eibhlín to elope with him.
It exists in many versions—not all of which could be deemed to
be translations. The version given here is by Gerald Griffin,
who wrote the novel* The Collegians, *which was the basis of
Boucicault's play* The Colleen Bawn *and of
Benedict's opera* The Lily of Killarney.

Le grá dhuit níl radharc am cheann, Eibhlín, a rún.
A' tracht ort is saibhreas liom, Eibhlín, a rún.
Mo mhórdháil ró ghrinn is tú,
Sólás an tsaoil is tú,
Ó, mo mheidhir is tú, mo ghreann is tú,
Mo bhruinneall thú go deimhin,
Is mo chlúr dá bhfuil sa choill sa is tú,
Is im' chroí istigh níl leigheas gan tú, Eibhlín, a rún.

Le cúirtéis nó clú 'bheathú, Eibhlín, a rún.
Dúirt bréag, nó ba liom féinig tú, Eibhlín, a rún.
Is breátha ná'n Vénus tú,
'S is áille ná'n réaltann tú,
Mo Helen tú gan bhéam.
Is tú mo rós, mo lil', mo chraobh,
Is mo stór dá bhfuil sa tsaol sa is tú,
Is rún mo chroí is mo chléibh is tú, Eibhlín, a rún.

Rachainn thar sáile leat, Eibhlín, a rún.
'S go deo, deo, ní fhágfainn thú, Eibhlín, a rún.
Le stárthaibh do bhréagfainn thú
'S do bhlaisfinn do bhéal go dlúth,
Do shínfinn go séimh led' chum,
Fé ghéaga glasa crann.
Thabharfainn aeraíocht duit cois abhann,
Agus ceol na n-éan os ár gceann, Eibhlín, a rún.

• • • • • • • • • • • • • • • •

When like the early rose,
Eileen aroon!
Beauty in childhood blows;
Eileen aroon!
When like a diadem,
Buds blush around the stem,
Which is the fairest gem?
Eileen aroon!

Is it the laughing eye,
Eileen aroon!
Is it the timid sigh,
Eileen aroon!
Is it the tender tone,
Soft as the string'd harp's moan?
Oh, it is the truth alone.
Eileen Aroon!

When, like the rising day,
Eileen aroon!
Love sends his early ray,
Eileen aroon!
What makes his dawning glow
Changeless through joy or woe?
Only the constant know—
Eileen aroon!

I knew a valley fair,
Eileen aroon!
I knew a cottage there,
Eileen aroon!
Far in that valley's shade
I knew a gentle maid,
Flower of a hazel glade,
Eileen aroon!

Róisín Dhubh
(Dark Rosaleen)

While this song probably originated as a simple love song, extra
verses were added in later years, and the name 'Róisín Dhubh'
came to stand for the image of Ireland. The translation
given is that of the early nineteenth-century poet
James Clarence Mangan.

A Róisín, ná bíodh brón ort, ná cás anois,
Tá na bráithre ag teacht thar sáile, 's ag triall ar muir,
Tiocfaidh do phardún ón Phápa, 's ón Róimh anoir,
'S ní sparálfar fíon na Spáinne ar mo Róisín Dhubh.

Tá lionn dubh ar na triúcha, agus ceo ar na cnoic,
Tá fraoch ar na sléibhte, 's ní hiónadh sin,
Do thaoscfainn an tréanmhuir i bplaosc an uibh,
Dá bhféadfainn a bheith réidh leat, mo Róisín Dhubh.

Beidh an fharraige 'na tuillte dearga, 's an spéir 'na fuil.
Beidh an saol 'na cogadh craorach de dhroim na gcnoc,
Beidh gach gleann sléibhe ar fud Éireann is móinte ar crith,
Lá éigin sula n-éagfaidh mo Róisín Dhubh.

• •

O my Dark Rosaleen,
    Do not sigh, do not weep!
The priests are on the ocean green,
    They march along the Deep.
There's wine … from the royal Pope
    Upon the ocean green;
And Spanish ale shall give you hope,
    My Dark Rosaleen!

My own Rosaleen!
Shall glad your heart, shall give you hope,
Shall give you health, and help, and hope,
    My Dark Rosaleen.

Over hills and through dales,
    Have I roamed for your sake;
All yesterday I sailed with sails
    On river and on lake.
The Erne ... at its highest flood
    I dashed across unseen,
For there was lightning in my blood,
    My Dark Rosaleen!
    My own Rosaleen!
Oh! there was lightning in my blood,
Red lightning lightened through my blood,
    My Dark Rosaleen!

All day long in unrest
    To and fro do I move,
The very soul within my breast
    Is wasted for you, love!
The heart ... in my bosom faints
    To think of you, my Queen,
My life of life, my saint of saints,
    My Dark Rosaleen!
    My own Rosaleen!
To hear your sweet and sad complaints,
My life, my love, my saint of saints,
    My Dark Rosaleen!

Woe and pain, pain and woe,
    Are my lot night and noon,
To see your bright face clouded so,
    Like to the mournful moon.
But yet ... will I rear your throne
    Again in golden sheen;
'Tis you shall reign, shall reign alone,

My Dark Rosaleen!
My own Rosaleen!
'Tis you shall have the golden throne,
'Tis you shall reign, and reign alone,
My Dark Rosaleen!

Over dews, over sands
Will I fly for your weal;
Your holy delicate white hands
Shall girdle me with steel.
At home … in your emerald bowers,
From morning's dawn till e'en,
You'll pray for me, my flower of flowers,
My Dark Rosaleen!
My fond Rosaleen!
You'll think of me through daylight's hours,
My virgin flower, my flower of flowers,
My Dark Rosaleen!

I could scale the blue air,
I could plough the high hills,
Oh, I could kneel all night in prayer,
To heal your many ills!
And one … beamy smile from you
Would float like light between
My toils and me, my own, my true,
My Dark Rosaleen!
My fond Rosaleen!
Would give me life and soul anew,
A second life, a soul anew,
My Dark Rosaleen!

Úna Bhán

*This song, or lament, sprang from a tragic situation
aggravated by foolish male pride. Tomás Láidir Costello, a late
seventeenth-century poet, had fallen in love with Úna, the
daughter of rich parents who forbade the two to meet.
Úna, however, fell into a wasting love-sickness, and Tomás was
invited to visit her; his presence so comforted her that she fell
into the first sound sleep she had experienced for many days.
Tomás decided that while she was asleep he should leave her, for
fear of compromising her. On his way home he vowed that he
would not return unless he was summoned before he crossed a
certain river. Although he delayed for over half an hour on the
river-bank, no summons came until he had crossed the river; it
was only then that the messenger came. Tomás refused to break
his vow and did not return. Poor Úna, overcome with
sorrow, died; Tomás, in his turn, was overcome with grief and
composed this lament for his lost love.
The translation given below is by Seán Mac Mathghamhna.*

Na cheithre Úna, na cheithre Áine, na cheithre Máire 's
    na cheithre Nóra,
Na cheithre mná ba cheithre breácha i gceithre gcearda na
    Fódhla,
Na cheithre táirní a chuaidh 's na cheithre clára, na cheithre
    cláracha cónra,
Ach na cheithre gráin ar na cheithre mná nach dtug na cheithre
    grá go na cheithre póga.

'Gus 'Úna Bhán nic Diarmaid Óig,
Fíorsgoth Búrcach, Brúnach, 's Brianach Mór,
Bhí do bhéal mar an tsiúcra, mar leamhnacht, mar fhíon, 's
    mar bheoir,
'Gus do chois deas lúfar 'sí shiúlfadh gan fiar i mbróig.

69

A shúil is glaise Ó ná ligean anuas an bhraon,
A ghuth is binne ná guth na cuaiche ar chraobh,
A thaobh is gile Ó ná coipeadh na gcuan seo thíos,
'Gus a stór is a chumainn, nach minic do bhuaireadh thríom.

• •

The four Únas, the four Áines, the four Máires, the four Nóras,
The four women finest by fourfold in the four quarters of Fódhla,
The four nails driven into the four coffin boards, the four
    oak coffins O;
But my fourfold hate on the four women who gave not their love
    with their kisses four.

Fair Úna, daughter of Diarmuid Óg,
Choicest flower of the Burkes, Brownes, and lordly O'Briens,
Your mouth was like honey, like milk, like wine,
And your slender foot faultlessly graced a shoe.

O eye clearer than the falling raindrop,
O voice sweeter than the cuckoo on the branch,
O side whiter than the foam of the raging sea,
O my treasure and my love, how often have your sorrows pierced
    me through.

Nothing I find as fair as my love,
Not even the fallen snow enmantled with blood.
And oh you women, were not one call for me at the ford
Better than all your wailing for Úna dead.

O Úna, rose in a garden,
Golden candlestick on a queen's table,
You were birdsong exultant and music to me,
My stricken grief not to have wed with you.

O little brother, if you had seen her in church,
Her hair adorned with green ribbon
In tresses of amber and gold,
But O my heavy sorrow: she was not betrothed to me.

I would go with you Úna on a raft or a boat,
O fair breast that knows no man yet,
But by the Holy Book I swear
Unless you be mine my head too will lie deep under the clay.

Pity that I were not as the raven
That could fly to Úna in her mansion on the hill,
Or that I were a sunbeam shining on the topmost branch and
    on the eddying stream,
I could be with my love everywhere.

Fair Úna how ugly now is your bed,
Your head lying among hosts of the dead.
Unless you come to me, even as a ghost, O flower without
    blemish,
Never again will I come to visit you after this night.

Dollaí Nic Dhonncha (Dolly MacDonagh)

This is a song by the celebrated early eighteenth-century poet and harper Turlough O'Carolan. A young O'Hara was in love with a lady called Dolly MacDonagh in County Sligo. The lady's family, however, discouraged him because of his lack of wealth. O'Carolan thought this was a great pity and wrote this song; O'Hara learned the song and constantly sang it under the maiden's window until her heart was conquered and she agreed to elope with him despite the disapproval of her family and friends. The translation given is by Douglas Hyde.

Go Craoibhí choíche má théann tú,
Dearc ar mhnaoi na bpéarla,
Deirionn bhán na mínrosc 's ní baol duit go deo,
Ba dheise a com ná an eala
Gan ghruaim gan chruas gan chráiteacht
'S a mala chaol tá tarraingte ó nádúr gan stró.

Ba ghile a píob 's bráid gheal
Ná sneachta mín dá charnadh,
'S ná an lile rug barr maise is breáchta ná an rós,
A dhrúcht na maidne is áille
An ghrian faoi smúit go bhfaigh' tú,
Ag éirí ar na hardaibh gach sármhaidin ceo.

· · · · · · · · · · · · · · · ·

To Crevagh if you ever go
Look at the girl of the pearls
The white [...] of the smooth eyes and there will never be
any fear of you.
Her shape was fairer than the swan's
With no gloom or hardness or penury,
And her narrow forehead that is drawn by Nature without
prodigality.

Her throat and her white neck were brighter
Than smooth snow being piled up
And than the lily which took the top of loveliness finer than
the rose.
Oh, dew of the morning most lovely,
That you may find the sun without a cloudlet
Rising over the heights, each splendid misty morning.

It is destroyed I am, and poor,
Lying in lack of health,
And my cure is not to be found with any leech alive.
My heart is being torn in pieces,
Like a sledge falling on iron;
Relieve me, God, or I will not be long here.

Oh, mouth that is narrow and darling,
Never do that to me,
Give to me a kiss or two, secretly, as a cure for my pain.
If you do that, without doubt
As long as the world and happiness shall last
I shall never part from thee; oh, my affection, my desire.

Like the dew of a summer morning
My delight was struck upon me,
Like the star of the morning rising, on the rising of day.
Oh, secret of my heart and my delight,
Understand not that I do not want thee
Though Rome and France were to be lost by it—steal off
  with me without delay.

It is discomfited and poor I am,
Lying in lack of health,
And my cure is not to be found with any leech alive.
Oh, secret of my heart who art friendly;
Oh, love of everyone who has seen thee,
Unless thou cross the sea with me I shall not be long alive.

Beití Ní Bhriain (Betty O'Brien)

This is another song by O'Carolan; this time, however, it was not composed to be used by a suitor but was intended, as so many of O'Carolan's pieces were, simply as a tribute to a person of noble birth—more often than not one of his patrons or sponsors. The translation, again, is by Douglas Hyde.

Tá stáidbhean Mumhan
Láimh le Buain
    Mar deir gach eolaí sármhaith,
'Sí Beití Ní Bhriain í,
Ainnir na gciabh í
    Cailín is sciamhaí gáire.
Cá fiú mé bheith beo,
Muna bhfaighidh mé póg
    Óna béal mar rós i ngairdín.
Dearbhaím féin duit
Dá mbeadh sí san Éigipt
    Go rachainn ag féachaint a háille.

• • • • • • • • • • • • • •

There is a stately woman of Munster,
Nigh unto the Boyne,
    As each good learned-man says,
She is Betty O'Brian,
The maiden of the locks,
    The girl of most lovely laugh,
How is it worth while for me to be alive
Unless I shall get a kiss
    From her mouth like a rose in a garden?
I myself assert it to you
That if she were in Egypt
    I would go to look at her beauty.

The mild woman, sunny, shapely,
    The sister of O'Brian and MacCarthy,
Whosoever would sit by her side
And would kiss her mouth,
    Life and health were near to him.
I placed delight
In the back of ringlets,
    By which I have lost activity and health.
Sleep in the night
I do not get for want of her,
Without my being constantly near her.

Oh, Betty of the mild eyes,
Who hast led astray every province,
    You, with whom the thousands are in love,
The riches of Greece
I would not accept at all
    If I got my choice of being betrothed to you,
Oh, plant of the true blood
And sister of kings,
    With whom the world is in love and affection,
How you are like to Deirdre,
Oh, darling of the women of Erin,
    Oh, lily, who won the victory for loveliness,

Oh, sister of the secret
Do not do that,
    But with the inclining of your eye give me relief,
Keep me from the death,
Let you yourself have me,
    And I shall be merry and pleased.
The county of Leitrim of the welcomes, Sligo,
And full-right Antrim—
A kiss of your mouth,
Sure it were dearer to myself
    Than all that put together and let me get it.

Dónall Óg (Young Donal)

This has been described as 'a song that cannot be surpassed for simplicity, softness, gentleness and deep sorrow.' Of the girl who composed the song originally nothing is known except that, as the song reveals, she was deserted by Donal. The translation is by Seán Mac Mathghamhna.

A Dhónaill Óig má théighir thar farraige
Tabhair mé féin leat 's ná déan do dhearmad,
Beidh agat féirín lá aonaigh agus margaidh
Agus iníon Rí Gréige mar chéile leaptha agat.

Gheall tú dhomsa agus rinne tú bréag liom
Go mbeitheá romhamsa ag cró na gcaorach;
Lig mé fead agus dhá bhlaoi dhéag ort
'S ní raibh romham ach na huain agus iad a méilí.

Siúd é an Domhnach a dtug mé grá dhuit,
A' Domhnach díreach roimh Domhnach Cásca,
Is tú ar do ghlúine ag léamh na Páise
Sea bhí mo dhá shúil a, síorthabhairt grá dhuit.

• • • • • • • • • • • • • • • •

O Donal Óg, if over the sea you go
Take me with you and do not forsake me.
You shall have a gift every fair and market day
And the daughter of the King of Greece for wife.

You promised but told me a lie
That you would meet me at the sheep-shed.
I whistled and called again and again—
No answer but lambs sadly bleating.

That was the Sunday I gave my heart to you,
The Sunday before Easter Sunday,
You on your knees reading the Passion
And my eyes love-consuming you.

When I visit Patrick's holy well
Doing the Pattern for my fair love's sake
I no longer expect you to-day or to-morrow
And O my darling, farewell wherever you are.

When I visit Brigid's well
And sit down to rest a while,
My eyes well up and flood with tears;
Dark thoughts make grey my dark head.

When I visit the house of merriment
I sit down in sorrow;
I see every one but my own one
Whose amber locks curled to his cheek.

O fairest of the fair, O reddest of the red haired,
Brightest star of all the world, you left me in sorrow;
When I hear other women named with your name
My hair falls out right to the very root.

My heart is as black as the sloe,
Or black coal in a smith's forge,
Or black shoes on lime-white halls
And a black cloud of sorrow overhangs my laughter.

You've taken East from me, you've taken West from me,
You've taken the future and the past from me,
You've taken the Moon from me, you've taken the Sun from me
And great is my fear you've taken God from me.

Nóra Ní Chonchúir Bháin (Nóra, Daughter of O'Connor the Fair)

*This song is the expression of a man's grief at the fact that the
woman he loved has married another. The translation
is by Seán Mac Mathghamhna.*

Is fad' ó fuair mé faill ar chailín óg sa ngleann
Agus geallúint ar í fháil l'aghaidh pósadh,
Ach mo chreach agus mo chrá, ní dhom a bhí sí i ndán
Ach don té udaigh nár tráchtaíodh fós air!

Nach é do chumann a bhí gearr a chlis orm 's gach áit
Nó go síntear mé 'gus tú i gcláraí cóntra,
Ach a Nór' Ní Chonchúir Bháin sí do phóg ba mhian liom fháil,
Nó an bhfuil tú le bheith i ndán go deo dhom.

Agus thug mé searc is gnaoi do chailín óg sa tír
Mar is ormsa bhí dith mór na céille,
Is go bhfuil fhios ag a' saol 's ag an mbaile siúd a mbím
Go leanfainn stór mo chroí dhá bhféadfainn.

• • • • • • • • • • • • • • • • •

I could have had long ago
The young girl from the glen as my promised bride,
But my woe and my sorrow she was not to be mine
But his whose name is yet unspoken.

Our love's course was difficult and short,
Yet until we are laid out and coffined
O Nóra Ní Chonchúir Bháin for your kisses I will yearn
Or are you fated ever to be mine.

I gave love and affection to a young girl,
For great was my lack of sense
And the whole world as my own village knows
That I would follow my love to the end of all.

And is there any affliction worse than love,
Though death at will can scatter multitudes;
But glory to the King of Grace such is not my state,
For soon my marriage will be arranged.

And but for those lying folk I would go to you
Every morning and every evening too.
Pity me then looking for you
And not knowing, despite careful searching, where you are.

Vain as a letter addressed to a tomb is my seeking for you
And I cannot forget the pain you caused,
But O dearest treasure of my heart
Fare thee well since we cannot marry.

O early and late my eye overflows with tears
And I heave many a sigh on account of you
And the whole world as my own village knows
That I would follow you wherever you would go.

I shall not live a month with sorrow lying heavy on my heart
And I do not mind whatever place you may find;
But in the tavern I shall not be found nor anywhere around
For I am saying goodbye to the young of this world.

Caoineadh Airt Uí Laoghaire (The Lament for Art O'Leary)

The background to this powerful lament is highly complex and, in essence, political. In 1767 the marriage of O'Leary to Eibhlín Dhubh Ní Chonaill was strongly opposed by her family. In a county, Cork, notorious for the readiness of its magistrates to keep the penal laws alive, O'Leary had had several brushes with the law. A magistrate called Morris, provoked by O'Leary's assertiveness, demanded a horse of his in exchange for five pounds (this being the maximum value for a horse owned by a Catholic). There was then an incident involving O'Leary's seizing of a gun from Morris, which was a grave violation of the law; the outcome was that eventually O'Leary was shot dead by soldiers accompanying Morris in 1773—a crime for which Morris was subsequently tried for murder and found guilty. The lament traditionally was composed by Eibhlín on the very spot on which Art was slain. There is a short version, likely to have been the original, and a longer version: both are given here. The first translation is by Máirín Ní Dhonnchadha; the longer is by Frank O'Connor.

Mo chara gu daingan tu, du thug mo shúil aire duit,
Du thug mo croidhe taithnamh duit is d'éláíghus óm' charaid leat
Is dam-sa nár bh'aitrach Du chuiris párlús dá gheladh dhom
Seombraidhe dá nglanadh dham Bácús dá dhergadh dham
Bríc dá cepadh dham Róst dá bhrecadh dham
Riaradh is glacadh dam Búird dá lethadh dham
Fíon dá tharang dham Mairt dá legadh dham
Muca dá bh-fedadh dham Mná fuinnach rennta dham
Mná glactha lestair dham Codhladh i g-clúmh lachan dam
Gu d-tighadh andsh edartha Nó tharis dá d-aithnach lium
Cia gur b'é lethag ort Má bhídhtá cecartha
Ní bhídhtá acht tamall beg. Badh mise fá ndera san
Tá fhios ag an Athair-Mhac Gur m-b'iu fear dush ainime
súd do mhaitamh duit A mharcaigh an Mhallda-roisg.

Mo chara gu daingan tu Is breagh thighadh hata duit
Faoi bhannda d'ór thairaingthe is cloidhamh cínn airgaid
Coiscéim bhalarach ag each cael cennan fughat
D'umhalaighidís Sagsanaig Síos gu talamh duit
is ní air mhaithadh let Acht le h-aen chorp egla
Cia gur leo caillag tu.

A mharcaig na m-bán-ghlac Is breágh thighach ráib duit
Solón faoi cháimbric A's hata faoi lása
Tar éis techt tar sáile Glantí andsh shráid dhuit
A's ní le grádh duit Acht le h-aen-chorp gráin ort.

Mo chara tu gu daingan is 'n uair thiocfidh chugham-sa i bhaile
Conchabhar beg an chena is Fear Ó Laeghaire an lenbh
Fiafreoighidh diom go tapa Cár 'fhágbhas fein a n-athair
Inneosad dóibh faoi mhairg gur fhágbhas i g-Cíll na Martar
Glaeidhfidh siad ar a n-athar is ní bheidh sé agtha le fregairt

• •

Steadfast love! my eye followed you,
my heart loved you, and I stole away from my kin with you.
I never regretted it. You had a parlour made bright for me,
rooms cleaned for me, an oven reddened for me

loafbread shaped for me, roast meat dressed for me,
tending and waiting on me, tables laid for me,
wine strained for me, cattle felled for me,
pigs' throats stuck for me, women who'd cook cuts for me,
vessel-fetching women for me, sleeping in duck-down for me,
until the milking-time came, or later if I pleased.
Although that tale was spread of you, if ever you were niggardly,
it was only for a short spell, and then the fault was mine;
the Father-Son knows that a man of your name
deserves to be forgiven that much, horseman of the slow eye.

My steadfast love, how well a hat looked on you
with its band of drawn gold, and a silver-hilted sword,
on a slender, white-headed horse, cantering.
The Saxons used scrape the ground before you
and not to show you any favour, but from sheer dread of you—
though it was to them you lost your life.

Horseman of the white hands, how well a blade suited you
a holland-shirt with cambric handkerchief, and a hat with lace.
When you came home from overseas, people fled the street
    before you—
and not for love of you, but from sheer dislike!

My steadfast love, when they'll come home to me—
darling little Conchubhar, and the baby, Fear Ó Laoghaire,
they'll ask me straight away where did I leave their daddy,
I'll tell them in my anguish that I left him in Cill na Martar,
they'll call out to their daddy and he'll not be there to answer.

• •

My love and my darling
The first day I saw you
By the market-house gable,
My eye was watching you,
My heart adoring you,
I fled from my father with you,
Far from my home with you.

No grievous choice was mine,
For me you made all fine,
Parlours were whitened for me,
Bedrooms painted for me,
Ovens reddened for me,
Loaves baked for me,
Roast spitted for me,
Beeves slaughtered for me,
Beds made for me,
There was sleep on down for me
Till milking time came round
And later if I pleased.

My mind remembers
That bright spring day,
How a hat with a band of gold became you,
A sword silver-hilted,
A manly right hand,
A menacing prancing,
A shudder of fear
On the foes about you;
For when you passed riding
On your white-nosed mare
The English bowed
To the ground before you,
Out of no love for you,
Out of their fear,
Though sweetheart of my soul,
The English killed you.

Rider of the white palm,
How a brooch became you
In a shirt of cambric!
And your hat with laces—
When you rode there,
And their streets were bare,
'Twas no love that stayed them
But hatred and fear.

My love and my calf
Of the race of the earls of Antrim
And the Barrys of Eemokilly,
A sword became you.
A hat with a band,
A slender foreign shoe
And a suit of yarn
Woven over the water.

My love and my secret
'Tis well you were suited
In a five-ribbed stocking
Your legs top-booted,
Your cornered Caroline
Your cracking whip.
Your sprightly gelding—
Oh, many's the girl
That would stop to behold you!

My love and my sweetheart,
When I come back
Little pet Conor
And Fiach the baby
Will ask me surely
Where I left their father;
I will say with anguish
'Twas in Kilnamartyr—
They will call the father
That will never answer.

My love and my darling
That I never thought dead
Till your horse came to me
With bridle trailing,
All blood from forehead
To polished saddle
Where you should be,
Sitting or standing;

I gave one leap to the threshold,
A second to the gate,
A third upon her back.

I clapped my hands
And galloped wildly
Fast as I could ride her
Till I found you dead
By a little furze-bush,
Without pope or bishop
Or priest or cleric
One prayer to whisper,
But an old, old woman
And her cloak about you,
And your blood in torrents,
Art O'Leary,
I did not wipe it up,
I cupped it in my hands.

My love and my delight,
Rise up now beside me,
And let me lead you home!
Till we kill beeves for you,
And roast your meat for you,
Till we call company
And many a harper in;
And I shall make your bed
Of soft and snowy sheets,
And blankets dark and rough
To warm the lovely limbs
An autumn blast has chilled.

[*His sister speaks*]
My little love, my calf!
Here is a vision
That last night brought me,
In Cork all lonely
On my bed sleeping;

That the snowy court fell
And the enchanted castle
That we two played in
As children together;
Ballingeary withered,
And your hounds were silent,
Your birds were songless,
The while they found you
On the open mountain
Without priest or cleric
But an old, old woman,
And her coat about you,
When the earth caught you,
Art O'Leary,
And your life-blood stiffened
The white shirt on you.

My love and my treasure!
What fine lovely lady
From Cork of the white sails
To the Bridge of Toime
With her dowry gathered
And her cows at pasture
Would sleep alone
The night they waked you?

[*Eileen O'Connell replies*]
My love forever!
Never believe her
Her evil rumours;
'Tis a liar's story
That I slept while others
Sat round and waked you—
'Twas no sleep that took me
But the children crying:
They would not close their eyes
Without me beside them.

Oh, people, do not believe
Any lying story!
There is no woman in Ireland
That had slept beside him
And borne him three children
But would go wild
After Art O'Leary
That lies dead before me
Since yesterday morning.

Grief on you, Morris!
Heart's blood and bowel's blood!
May your eyes go blind
And your knees be broken!
You killed my darling
And no man in Ireland
Will fire the shot at you!

Blight and loss on you,
Morris the traitor!
That took my man from me,
My three children's father;
There are two on the hearth
And one in the womb
I shall not bring forth.

My love and my sweetness,
Art, rise up to me,
And leap upon your mare,
And ride into Macroom
And Inchigeela beyond,
Clasping your flask of wine,
One going, one coming back,
As in your father's time.

My grief, my destruction
That I was not by you
When the shot was fired
That my dress might hinder

My heart might hold it,
While you fled to the hills,
Rider of the ready hands.

My love and my fortune,
'Tis an evil portion
To lay for a giant,
A shroud and a coffin;
For a big-hearted hero
That fished in the hill-streams,
And drank in bright halls
With white-breasted women.

My love and my delight,
As you went out the gate,
You turned and hurried back,
And kissed your handsome sons,
And came and kissed my hand.
You said 'Eileen, rise up,
And set your business straight,
For I am leaving home,
I never may return.'
I laughed at what you said,
You had said as much before.

But my friend and my treasure,
My white-sworded rider,
Rise you from this slumber!
Put your best clothes on,
Of cloth new and noble.
Your hat of fine beaver,
On with your gauntlets!

Yonder hangs your whip!
Your horse is at the door,
Follow the small road east
Where every bush will bend
And every stream dry up,
And man and woman bow

If things have manners yet
That have them not I fear.

My love and my sweetheart,
'Tis not my people's death,
'Tis not my children's death
Nor Donal Mor O'Connell,
Conal that died by drowning
Nor the girl of six and twenty
That went across the water
To be a king's companion,
'Tis not all these I speak of
And call on with voice broken

But noble Art O'Leary,
Art of hair so golden,
Art of wit and courage,
Art the brown mare's master,
Swept last night to nothing
Here in Carraig an Ime—
Perish its name and people!

My love and my treasure,
My bright dove, my sweetheart,
Though I bring with me
No throng of mourners
'Tis no shame for me,
For my kinsmen are wrapped in
A sleep beyond waking,
In narrow coffins
Walled up in stone.

Though but for the smallpox
And the black death
And the spotted fever,
That host of riders
With bridles shaking
Would rouse the echoes,
Coming to your waking,
Art of the white breast!

Ay, could calls but reach and waken
Derrynane across the mountains,
Capling of the yellow apples,
Many a proud and stately rider,
Many a girl with spotless kerchief
Would be here before tomorrow,
Shedding tears about your body,
Art O'Leary once so merry!

My love and my secret,
Your corn is well stacked,
Your cows are at milking;
On me is the grief
There's no cure for in Munster.
Till Art O'Leary rise
This grief will never yield
That's bruising all my heart,
Yet shut up fast in it,
As 'twere in a locked trunk
With the key gone astray
And rust grown on the wards.

My love and my calf!
Noble Art O'Leary,
Son of Conor, son of Cady,
Son of Lewis O'Leary,
West of the Valley,
And east of Greenan
(Where berries grow thickly
And nuts crowd on branches,
And apples in heaps fall
In their own season)
What wonder to any
If Iveleary lighted
And Ballingeary,
And Gugan of the saints
For the smooth-palmed rider
The huntsman unwearied

That I would see spurring
From Grenagh without halting
When quick hounds had faltered?
Oh, rider of the bright eyes
What happened you yesterday?
I thought you in my heart
When I bought you your fine clothes
One the world could not slay.

My love and my delight,
Kin of the hardy horsemen
That would hunt all the glens
Till you had turned them home
And led them to the hall
Where tables would be spread,
Sharpness being put on knives,
Roasted beef being cut,
Bacon fit to eat,
Many a rib of mutton,
Oats in plenty hanging
To set the horses neighing—
Hairy slender horses
Flanked with sturdy horseboys,
Never charged their lodging,
Nor their horses' feeding
Had they stopped a fortnight.

'Tis known to Jesus Christ
Nor cap upon my head
Nor shift against my side
Nor shoe upon my foot
Nor gear in all my house
Nor bridle for the mare
But I will spend at law;
And I'll go oversea
And plead it with the king,
And if the king be deaf
No fear but I'll come back

To the black-blooded thief
That slew my man on me.

Oh, rider of the white palms,
Go you to Baldwin,
And face the schemer,
The bandy-legged monster
And take satisfaction
For your mare that he claimed.
May his six children rot!
(Wishing no harm to Maire
Yet of no love for her,
But that my mother's body
Was a bed to her for three seasons
And to me beside her).

My heart's love go to you,
Dark women of the Mill
For the sharp rhymes ye shed
On the rider of the brown mare—

But cease your weeping now,
Women of the soft, wet eyes,
Till Art O'Leary drink,
Ere he go to the dark school,
No student of music or song,
A prop for the earth and the stone.

Mary Hynes

*This is by the blind travelling fiddler and folk-poet Antaine
Ó Reachtaire or 'Raftery', who died in 1835. Most of
his compositions were based on contemporary, often political,
events. The translation is by Frank O'Connor.*

Going to Mass by the heavenly mercy,
    The day was rainy, the wind was wild;
I met a lady beside Kiltartan
    And fell in love with the lovely child;
My conversation was smooth and easy,
    And graciously she answered me
'Raftery dear, 'tis yourself that's welcome,
    So step beside me to Ballylee.'

This invitation there was no denying,
    I laughed with joy and my poor heart beat;
We had but to walk across a meadow,
    And in her dwelling I took my seat.
There was laid a table with a jug and glasses,
    And that sweet maiden sat down by me—
'Raftery drink and don't spare the liquor;
    There's a lengthy cellar in Ballylee.'

If I should travel France and England,
    And Spain and Greece and return once more
To study Ireland to the northern ocean,
    I would find no morsel the like of her.
If I was married to that youthful beauty
    I'd follow her through the open sea,
And wander coasts and winding roads
    With the shining pearl of Ballylee.

'Tis fine and bright on the mountainside,
    Looking down on Ballylee,
You can walk the woods, picking nuts and berries,
    And hear the birds sing merrily;
But where's the good if you got no tidings
    Of the flowering branch that resides below—
O summer sky, there's no denying
    It is for you that I ramble so.

My star of beauty, my sun of autumn,
    My golden hair, O my share of life!
Will you come with me this coming Sunday
    And tell the priest you will be my wife?
I'd not grudge you music, nor a feast at evening,
    Nor punch nor wine, if you'd have it be,
And King of Glory, dry up the roadway
    Till I find my posy at Ballylee!

— PART TWO

Anglo-Irish

The Recruiting Officer

Written by George Farquhar and first produced in 1707, this play has the distinction of being the first play staged in North America, in 1732, and in Australia, in 1789. Its author was born in Derry in 1677 or 1678. The piece chosen is from act 1.

WORTHY. Thou art a happy fellow; once I was so.

PLUME. What ails thee, man? No inundations nor earthquakes in Wales, I hope? Has your father rose from the dead, and reassumed his estate?

WORTHY. No.

PLUME. Then, you are married surely.

WORTHY. No.

PLUME. Then you are mad, or turning Quaker.

WORTHY. Come, I must out with it. Your once gay, roving friend is dwindled into an obsequious, thoughtful, romantic, constant coxcomb.

PLUME. And pray, what is all this for?

WORTHY. For a woman.

PLUME. Shake hands brother, if thou go to that. Behold me as obsequious, as thoughtful, and as constant a coxcomb as your worship.

WORTHY. For whom?

PLUME. For a regiment. But for a woman! 'Sdeath, I have been constant to fifteen at a time, but never melancholy for one; and can the love of one bring you into this pickle? Pray, who is this miraculous Helen?

WORTHY. A Helen indeed, not to be won under a ten years' siege; as great a beauty, and as great a jilt.

PLUME. A jilt! Pho! Is she as great a whore?

WORTHY. No, no.

PLUME. 'Tis ten thousand pities. But who is she? Do I know her?

WORTHY. Very well.

PLUME. That's impossible. I know no woman that will hold out a ten years' siege.

WORTHY. What think you of Melinda?

PLUME. Melinda! Why, she began to capitulate this time twelvemonth, and offered to surrender upon honourable terms; and I advised you to propose a settlement of five hundred pound a year to her, before I went last abroad.

WORTHY. I did, and she hearkened to't, desiring only one week to consider; when, beyond her hopes, the town was relieved, and I forced to turn my siege into a blockade.

PLUME. Explain, explain.

WORTHY. My lady Richly (her aunt in Flintshire) dies, and leaves her at this critical time twenty thousand pound.

PLUME. O the devil, what a delicate woman was there spoiled! But by the rules of war now, Worthy, blockade was foolish. After such a convoy of provisions was entered the place, you could have no thought of reducing it by famine. You should have redoubled your attacks, taken the town by storm, or have died upon the breach.

WORTHY. I did make one general assault, and pushed it with all my forces; but I was so vigorously repulsed, that despairing of ever gaining her for a mistress, I have altered my conduct, given my addresses the obsequious and distant turn, and court her now for a wife.

PLUME. So, as you grew obsequious, she grew haughty, and because you approached her as a goddess, she used you like a dog.

WORTHY. Exactly.

PLUME. 'Tis the way of 'em all. Come Worthy, your obsequious and distant airs will never bring you together; you must not think to surmount her pride by your humility. Would you bring her to better thoughts of you, she must be reduced to a meaner opinion of herself. Let me see. The very first thing that I would do, should be to lie with her chambermaid, and hire three or four wenches in the neighbourhood to report that I had got them with child. Suppose we lam-

pooned all the pretty women in town, and left her out?
Or what if we made a ball, and forgot to invite her, with one
or two of the ugliest?

WORTHY. These would be mortifications, I must confess; but we live
in such a precise, dull place, that we can have no balls, no
lampoons, no—

PLUME. What, no bastards! And so many recruiting officers in town;
I thought 'twas a maxim among them to leave as many
recruits in the country as they carried out.

WORTHY. Nobody doubts your goodwill, noble captain, in serving
your country with your best blood—witness our friend
Molly at the castle. There have been tears in town about
that business, captain.

PLUME. I hope Silvia has not heard of't.

WORTHY. O sir, have you thought of her? I began to fancy you had
forgot poor Silvia.

PLUME. Your affairs had put mine quite out of my head. 'Tis true,
Silvia and I had once agreed to go to bed together, could we
have adjusted preliminaries; but she would have the wedding before consummation, and I was for consummation
before the wedding. We could not agree; she was a pert,
obstinate fool, and would lose her maidenhead her own
way, so she may keep it for Plume.

WORTHY. But do you intend to marry upon no other conditions?

PLUME. Your pardon, sir, I'll marry upon no conditions at all; if I
should, I'm resolved never to bind myself to a woman for
my whole life, till I know whether I shall like her company
for half an hour. Suppose I married a woman that wanted a
leg? Such a thing might be, unless I examined the goods
beforehand. If people would but try one another's constitu-
tions before they engaged, it would prevent all these elope-
ments, divorces, and the devil knows what.

Stella's Birthday, 1718

*Written in 1718 by Jonathan Swift on the occasion of
the birthday of Stella (Esther Johnson), with whom he had a
long-standing and rather unsatisfactory love affair.*

Stella this day is thirty-four,
(We shan't dispute a year or more:)
However Stella, be not troubled,
Although thy size and years are doubled,
Since first I saw thee at sixteen,
The brightest virgin on the green.
So little is thy form declined;
Made up so largely in thy mind.

Oh, would it please the gods to *split*
Thy beauty, size, and years, and wit,
No age could furnish out a pair
Of nymphs so graceful, wise and fair:
With half the lustre of your eyes,
With half your wit, your years, and size:
And then before it grew too late,
How should I beg of gentle fate,
(That either nymph might have her swain,)
To split my worship too in twain.

Stella's Birthday, 1727

This was written on the occasion of Stella's birthday in 1727;
the gentle contrast with the previous poem is notable.

This day, whate'er the fates decree,
Shall still be kept with joy by me:
This day then, let us not be told,
That you are sick, and I grown old,
Nor think on our approaching ills,
And talk of spectacles and pills.
Tomorrow will be time enough
To hear such mortifying stuff.

Yet, since from reason may be brought
A better and more pleasing thought,
Which can in spite of all decays,
Support a few remaining days:
From not the gravest of divines,
Accept for once some serious lines.

Although we now can form no more
Long schemes of life, as heretofore;
Yet you, while time is running fast,
Can look with joy on what is past.

Were future happiness and pain,
A mere contrivance of the brain,
As atheists argue, to entice,
And fit their proselytes for vice;
(The only comfort they propose,
To have companions in their woes.)
Grant this the case, yet sure 'tis hard,
That virtue, styled its own reward,

And by all sages understood
To be the chief of human good,
Should acting, die, nor leave behind
Some lasting pleasure in the mind;
Which by remembrance will assuage,
Grief, sickness, poverty, and age;
And strongly shoot a radiant dart,
To shine through life's declining part.

Say, Stella, feel you no content,
Reflecting on a life well spent?
Your skilful hand employed to save
Despairing wretches from the grave;
And then supporting with your store,
Those whom you dragged from death before:
(So Providence on mortals waits,
Preserving what it first creates)
Your generous boldness to defend
An innocent and absent friend;
That courage which can make you just,
To merit humbled in the dust:
The detestation you express
For vice in all its glittering dress:
That patience under torturing pain,
Where stubborn Stoics would complain.

Shall these, like empty shadows pass,
Or forms reflected from a glass?
Or mere chimeras in the mind,
That fly and leave no marks behind?
Does not the body thrive and grow
By food of twenty years ago?
And, had it not been still supplied,
It must a thousand times have died.
Then, who with reason can maintain,
That no effects of food remain?
And, is not virtue in mankind
The nutriment that feeds the mind?

Upheld by each good action past,
And still continued by the last:
Then, who with reason can pretend,
That all effects of virtue end?

Believe me Stella, when you show
That true contempt for things below,
Nor prize your life for other ends
Than merely to oblige your friends;
Your former actions claim their part,
And join to fortify your heart.
For virtue in her daily race,
Like Janus, bears a double face;
Looks back with joy where she has gone,
And therefore goes with courage on.
She at your sickly couch will wait,
And guide you to a better state.

O then, whatever heaven intends,
Take pity on your pitying friends;
Nor let your ills affect your mind,
To fancy they can be unkind.
Me, surely me, you ought to spare,
Who gladly would your sufferings share;
Or give my scrap of life to you,
And think it far beneath your due;
You, to whose care so oft I owe,
That I'm alive to tell you so.

A Prayer for Stella

This is the third of three prayers composed by Swift and used by him at Stella's bedside during her fatal illness. All three attest to the quality of his devotion to her, of his religion, and of his style at its most personal. This one was composed in November 1727.

O Merciful Father, who never afflictest thy Children, but for their own Good, and with Justice, over which thy Mercy always prevaileth, either to turn them to Repentance, or to punish them in the present Life in order to reward them in a better; take Pity, we beseech thee, upon this thy poor afflicted Servant, languishing so long and so grievously under the Weight of thy Hand. Give her strength, O Lord, to support her Weakness; and Patience to endure her Pains, without repining at thy Correction. Forgive every rash and inconsiderate Expression, which her Anguish may at any Time force from her Tongue, while her Heart continueth in an entire Submission to thy Will. Suppress in her, O Lord, all eager Desires of Life, and lessen her Fears of Death, by inspireing into her an humble, yet assured, Hope of thy Mercy. Give her a sincere Repentance for all her Transgressions and Omissions, and a firm Resolution to pass the Remainder of her Life in endeavouring to her utmost to observe all they Precepts. We beseech thee, likewise, to compose her Thoughts; and preserve to her the Use of her Memory and Reason during the course of her Sickness. Give her a true Conception of the Vanity, Folly, and Insignificancy of all human Things; and strengthen her so as to beget in her a sincere Love of thee in the Midst of her Sufferings. Accept, and impute, all her good Deeds; and forgive her all those Offences against thee, which she hath sincerely repented of, or through the Frailty of Memory hath forgot. And now, O Lord, we turn to thee, in Behalf of ourselves and the rest of her sorrowful Friends. Let not our Grief afflict her Mind, and thereby have an ill Effect on her present Distempers. Forgive the Sorrow and Weakness of those among us, who sink under the Grief and Terror of losing so dear and useful a Friend. Accept and pardon our most earnest Prayers and Wishes for her longer Continuance in this evil World, to do what thou art pleased to call thy Service, which is only her bounden Duty; that she may be still a Comfort to us, and to all others who will want the benefit of her Conversation, her Advice, her good Offices, or her Charity. And since thou hast promised, that where two or three are gathered together in thy Name, thou wilt be in the midst of them, to grant their Request; O gracious Lord, grant to us, who are here met in thy Name, that those Requests, which in the utmost Sincerity and Earnestness of our Hearts we have now made in behalf of this thy distressed Servant and of ourselves, may effectually be answered; through the Merits of Jesus Christ our Lord. Amen.

The Vicar of Wakefield

The opening paragraphs of this novel, written by Oliver Goldsmith and published in 1766, display a gentle maturity at contrast with the dramatic works of other Irish writers of the period.

I was ever of opinion that the honest man who married and brought up a large family did more service than he who continued single and only talked of population. From this motive, I had scarce taken orders a year before I began to think seriously of matrimony, and chose my wife, as she did her wedding-gown, not for a fine glossy surface, but such qualities as would wear well. To do her justice, she was a good-natured, notable woman; and as for breeding, there were few country ladies who could show more. She could read any English book without much spelling; but for pickling, preserving, and cookery, none could excel her. She prided herself also upon being an excellent contriver in housekeeping; though I could never find that we grew richer with all her contrivances.

However, we loved each other tenderly, and our fondness increased as we grew old. There was, in fact, nothing that could make us angry with the world or each other. We had an elegant house, situated in a fine country, and a good neighbourhood. The year was spent in a moral or rural amusement; in visiting our rich neighbours and relieving such as were poor. We had no revolutions to fear nor fatigues to undergo; all our adventures were by the fireside, and all our migrations from the blue bed to the brown.

She Stoops to Conquer

Although this play of Oliver Goldsmith's is a rather rumbustious one, this conversation between Hardcastle and his wife shows the same kind of maturity witnessed in the extract from The Vicar of Wakefield. *Mrs Hardcastle has just remarked that she hates 'old-fashioned trumpery';*
Hardcastle replies:

HARDCASTLE. And I love it. I love everything that's old: old friends, old times, old manners, old books, old wine; and, I believe, Dorothy [*taking her hand*], you'll own I have been pretty fond of an old wife.

MRS HARDCASTLE. Lord, Mr Hardcastle, you're for ever at your Dorothys and your old wifes. You may be a Darby, but I'll be no Joan, I promise you. I'm not so old as you'd make me, by more than one good year. Add twenty to twenty, and make money of that.

HARDCASTLE. Let me see; twenty added to twenty, makes just fifty and seven!

MRS HARDCASTLE. It's false, Mr Hardcastle: I was but twenty when I was brought to bed of Tony, that I had by Mr Lumpkin, my first husband; and he's not come to years of discretion yet.

HARDCASTLE. Nor ever will, I dare answer for him. Ay, you have taught *him* finely!

MRS HARDCASTLE. No matter, Tony Lumpkin has a good fortune. My son is not to live by his learning. I don't think a boy wants much learning to spend fifteen hundred a year.

HARDCASTLE. Learning, quotha! A mere composition of tricks and mischief!

MRS HARDCASTLE. Humour, my dear: nothing but humour. Come, Mr Hardcastle, you must allow the boy a little humour.

HARDCASTLE. I'd sooner allow him a horse-pond! If burning the footmen's shoes, frightening the maids, and worrying the kittens, be humour, he has it. It was but yesterday he fastened my wig to the back of my chair, and when I went to make a bow, I popped my bald head in Mrs Frizzle's face!

This song was intended to be sung by Miss Hardcastle in
She Stoops to Conquer. *It was left out, apparently,*
because the lady who was playing Miss Hardcastle was the
owner of an inadequate voice.

Ah, me! when shall I marry me?
    Lovers are plenty; but fail to relieve me:
He, fond youth, that could carry me,
    Offers to love, but means to deceive me.

But I will rally, and combat the ruiner:
    Not a look, not a smile shall my passion discover:
She that gives all to the false one pursuing her,
    Makes but a penitent, loses a lover.

The Rivals

This play was written by the Dubliner Richard Brinsley
Sheridan and first staged in 1775. The epilogue sums up the
convolutions of the typical plots of the comedies of manners; the
extract from the play itself reveals them at work.

Ladies, for you—I heard our poet say—
He'd try to coax some moral from his play:
'One moral's plain,' cried I, 'without more fuss;
Man's social happiness all rests on us;
Through all the drama—whether damn'd or not—
Love gilds the scene, and women guide the plot.
From every rank obedience is our due—
D'ye doubt?—The world's great stage shall prove it true.'

    The cit, well skill'd to shun domestic strife,
Will sup abroad; but first he'll ask his wife:
John Trot, his friend, for once will do the same,
But then—he'll just step home to tell his dame.

    The surly squire at noon resolves to rule,
And half the day—Zounds! madam is a fool!
Convinced at night, the vanquished victor says,
Ah, Kate! you women have such coaxing ways.

    The jolly toper chides each tardy blade,
Till reeling Bacchus calls on Love for aid;
Then with each toast he sees fair bumpers swim.
And kisses Chloe on the sparkling brim!

    Nay, I have heard that statesmen—great and wise—
Will sometimes counsel with a lady's eyes!
The servile suitors watch her various face,
She smiles preferment, or she frowns disgrace,
Curtsies a pension here—there nods a place.

    Nor with less awe, in scenes of humbler life,
Is view'd the mistress, or is heard the wife.
The poorest peasant of the poorest soil,
The child of poverty, and heir to toil,
Early from radiant Love's impartial light
Steals one small spark to cheer this world of night:
Dear spark! that oft through winter's chilling woes
Is all the warmth his little cottage knows!

    The wandering tar, who not for years has press'd,
The widow'd partner of his day of rest,
On the cold deck, far from her arms removed,
Still hums the ditty which his Susan loved;

And while around the cadence rude is blown,
The boatswain whistles in a softer tone.
The soldier, fairly proud of wounds and toil,
Pants for the triumph of his Nancy's smile!
But ere the battle should he list her cries,
The lover trembles—and the hero dies!
That heart, by war and honour steel'd to fear,
Droops on a sigh, and sickens at a tear!
But ye more cautious, ye nice-judging few,
Who gave to beauty only beauty's due,
Though friends to love—ye view with deep regret
Our conquests marr'd, our triumphs incomplete,
Till polish'd wit more lasting charms disclose,
And judgment fix the darts which beauty throws!
In female breasts did sense and merit rule,
The lover's mind would ask no other school;
Shamed into sense, the scholars of our eyes,
Our beaux from gallantry would soon be wise;
Would gladly light, their homage to improve,
The lamp of knowledge at the torch of love!

• • • • • • • • • • • • • • • • • •

ABSOLUTE. By heavens! I shall forswear your company! You are the
most teasing, captious, incorrigible lover!—Do love like a
man.

FAULKLAND. I own I am unfit for company.

ABSOLUTE. Am I not a lover: ay, and a romantic one too? Yet do I
carry everywhere with me such a confounded farrago of
doubts, fears, hopes, wishes, and all the flimsy furniture of a
country miss's brain!

FAULKLAND. Ah! Jack, your heart and soul are not, like mine, fixed
immutably on one only object. You throw for a large stake,
but losing, you could stake and throw again;—but I have
set my sum of happiness on this cast, and not to succeed
were to be stripped of all.

ABSOLUTE. But, for heaven's sake! what grounds for apprehension
can your whimsical brain conjure up at present?

FAULKLAND. What grounds for apprehension, did you say? Heavens! are there not a thousand! I fear for her spirits—her health—her life!—My absence may fret her; her anxiety for my return, her fears for me, may oppress her gentle temper; and for her health, does not every hour bring me cause to be alarmed? If it rains, some shower may even then have chilled her delicate frame! If the wind be keen, some rude blast may have affected her! The heat of noon, the dews of the evening, may endanger the life of her for whom only I value mine. O Jack! when delicate and feeling souls are separated, there is not a feature in the sky, not a movement of the elements, not an aspiration of the breeze, but hints some cause for a lover's apprehension!

ABSOLUTE. Ay, but we may choose whether we will take the hint or not.—So, then Faulkland, if you were convinced that Julia were well and in spirits, you would be entirely content?

FAULKLAND. I should be happy beyond measure—I am anxious only for that.

ABSOLUTE. Then to cure your anxiety at once—Miss Melville is in perfect health, and is at this moment in Bath.

FAULKLAND. Nay, Jack—don't trifle with me.

ABSOLUTE. She is arrived here with my father within this hour.

FAULKLAND. Can you be serious?

ABSOLUTE. I thought you knew Sir Anthony better than to be surprised at a sudden whim of this kind.—Seriously, then, it is as I tell you—upon my honour.

FAULKLAND. My dear friend!—Hollo, Du-Peigne! my hat.—My dear Jack—now nothing on earth can give me a moment's uneasiness.

[*Re-enter Fag.*]

FAG. Sir, Mr Acres, just arrived, is below.

ABSOLUTE. Stay, Faulkland, this Acres lives within a mile of Sir Anthony, and he shall tell you how your mistress has been ever since you left her. Fag, show this gentleman up.

[*Exit Fag.*]

FAULKLAND. What, is he much acquainted in the family?

ABSOLUTE. Oh, very intimate: I insist on your not going: besides, his character will divert you.

FAULKLAND. Well, I should like to ask him a few questions.

ABSOLUTE. He is likewise a rival of mine—that is, of my other self's, for he does not think his friend Captain Absolute ever saw the lady in question; and it is ridiculous enough to hear him complain to me of one Beverley, a concealed skulking rival, who—

FAULKLAND. Hush!—he's here.

[*Enter Acres.*]

ACRES. Ha! my dear friend, noble captain, and honest Jack, how do'st thou? just arrived, faith, as you see.—Sir, your humble servant. Warm work on the roads, Jack!—Odds whips and wheels! I've travelled like a comet, with a tail of dust all the way as long as the Mall.

ABSOLUTE. Ah! Bob, you are indeed an eccentric planet, but we know your attraction hither.—Give me leave to introduce Mr Faulkland to you; Mr Faulkland, Mr Acres.

ACRES. Sir, I am most heartily glad to see you: sir, I solicit your connections.—Hey, Jack—what, this is Mr Faulkland, who—

ABSOLUTE. Ay, Bob, Miss Melville's Mr Faulkland.

ACRES. Odso! she and your father can be but just arrived before me?—I suppose you have seen them. Ah! Mr Faulkland, you are indeed a happy man.

FAULKLAND. I have not seen Miss Melville yet, sir;—I hope she enjoyed full health and spirits in Devonshire?

ACRES. Never knew her better in my life, sir,—never better. Odds blushes and blooms! she had been as healthy as the German Spa.

FAULKLAND. Indeed! I did hear that she has been a little indisposed.

ACRES. False, false, sir—only said to vex you: quite the reverse, I assure you.

FAULKLAND. There, Jack, you see she has the advantage of me; I had almost fretted myself ill.

ABSOLUTE. Now are you angry with your mistress for not having been sick?

FAULKLAND. No, no, you misunderstand me: yet surely a little trifling indisposition is not an unnatural consequence of absence from those we love.—Now confess—isn't there something unkind in this violent, robust, unfeeling health?

ABSOLUTE. Oh, it was very unkind of her to be well in your absence, to be sure!

ACRES. Good apartments, Jack.

FAULKLAND. Well, sir, but you were saying that Miss Melville has been so exceedingly well—what then she has been merry and gay, I suppose? Always in spirits—hey?

ACRES. Merry, odds crickets! she has been the belle and spirit of the company wherever she has been—so lively and entertaining! so full of wit and humour!

FAULKLAND. There, Jack, there.—Oh, by my soul! there is an innate levity in woman that nothing can overcome.—What! happy, and I away!

ABSOLUTE. Have done!—How foolish this is! just now you were only apprehensive for your mistress's spirits.

FAULKLAND. Why, Jack, have I been the joy and spirit of the company?

ABSOLUTE. No, indeed, you have not.

FAULKLAND. Have I been lively and entertaining?

ABSOLUTE. Oh, upon my word, I acquit you.

FAULKLAND. Have I been full of wit and humour?

ABSOLUTE. No, faith, to do you justice, you have been confoundedly stupid indeed.

ACRES. What's the matter with the gentleman?

ABSOLUTE. He is only expressing his great satisfaction at hearing that Julia has been so well and happy—that's all—hey, Faulkland?

FAULKLAND. Oh! I am rejoiced to hear it—yes, yes, she has a happy disposition!

ACRES. That she has indeed—then she is so accomplished—so sweet a voice—so expert at her harpsichord—such a mistress of flat and sharp, squallante, rumblante, and quiverante!— There was this time month—odds minums and crotchets! how she did chirrup at Mrs Piano's concert!

FAULKLAND. There again, what say you to this? you see she has been all mirth and song—not a thought of me!

ABSOLUTE. Pho! man, is not music the food of love?

FAULKLAND. Well, well, it may be so.—Pray, Mr—, what's his damned name?—Do you remember what songs Miss Melville sung?

ACRES. Not I indeed.

ABSOLUTE. Stay, now, they were some pretty melancholy purling-stream airs, I warrant; perhaps you may recollect;—did she sing, 'When absent from my soul's delight'?

ACRES. No, that wa'n't it.

ABSOLUTE. Or, 'Go, gentle dales'! [*Sings.*]

ACRES. Oh, no! nothing like it. Odds! now I recollect one of them—'My heart's my own, my will is free'. [*Sings.*]

FAULKLAND. Fool! fool that I am! to fix all my happiness on such a trifler! 'Sdeath! to make herself the pipe and ballad-monger of a circle to soothe her light heart with catches and glees!—What can you say to this, sir?

ABSOLUTE. Why, that I should be glad to hear my mistress had been so merry, sir.

FAULKLAND. Nay, nay, nay—I'm not sorry that she had been happy—no, no, I am glad of that—I would not have had her sad or sick—yet surely a sympathetic heart would have shown itself even in the choice of a song—she might have been temperately healthy, and somehow, plaintively gay;—but she has been dancing too, I doubt not!

ACRES. What does the gentleman say about dancing?

ABSOLUTE. He says the lady we speak of dances as well as she sings.

ACRES. Ay, truly, does she—there was at our last race ball—

FAULKLAND. Hell and the devil!—There!—there—I told you so! I told you so! Oh! she thrives in my absence!—Dancing! But her whole feelings have been in opposition with mine;—I have been anxious, silent, pensive, sedentary—my days have been hours of care, my nights of watchfulness.—She has been all health! spirit! laugh! song! dance!—Oh, damned, damned levity!

ABSOLUTE. For heaven's sake, Faulkland, don't expose yourself so!—

Suppose she has danced, what then?—does not the ceremony of society often oblige—

FAULKLAND. Well, well, I'll contain myself—perhaps as you say—for form sake.—What, Mr Acres, you were praising Miss Melville's manner of dancing a minuet—hey?

ACRES. Oh, I dare insure her for that—but what I was going to speak of was her country dancing. Odds swimmings! she has such an air with her!

FAULKLAND. Now disappointment on her!—Defend this, Absolute; why don't you defend this?—Country-dances! jigs and reels! am I to blame now? A minuet I could have forgiven—I should not have minded that—I say I should not have regarded a minuet—but country-dances! Zounds! had she made one in a cotillon—I believe I could have forgiven even that—but to be monkey-led for a night! to run the gauntlet through a string of amorous palming puppies!—to show paces like a managed filly!—Oh, Jack, there never can be but one man in the world whom a truly modest and delicate woman ought to pair with in a country-dance; and, even then, the rest of the couples should be her great-uncles and aunts!

ABSOLUTE. Ay, to be sure!—grandfathers and grandmothers!

FAULKLAND. If there be but one vicious mind in the set, 'twill spread like a contagion—the action of their pulse beats to the lascivious movement of the jig—their quivering, warm-breathed sighs impregnate the very air—the atmosphere becomes electrical to love, and each amorous spark darts through every link of the chain!—I must leave you—I own I am somewhat flurried—and that confounded looby has perceived it. [*Going.*]

ABSOLUTE. Nay, but stay, Faulkland, and thank Mr Acres for his good news.

FAULKLAND. Damn his news! [*Exit.*]

ABSOLUTE. Ha! ha! ha! poor Faulkland five minutes since—'nothing on earth could give him a moment's uneasiness!'

ACRES. The gentleman wa'n't angry at my praising his mistress, was he?

ABSOLUTE. A little jealous, I believe, Bob.

ACRES.   You don't say so? Ha! ha! jealous of me—that's a good joke.

ABSOLUTE. There's nothing strange in that, Bob! let me tell you, that
          sprightly grace and insinuating manner of yours will do
          some mischief among the girls here.

ACRES.   Ah! you joke—ha! ha! mischief—ha! ha! but you know I
          am not my own property, my dear Lydia has forestalled me.
          She could never abide me in the country, because I used to
          dress so badly—but odds frogs and tambours! I shan't take
          matters so here, now ancient madam has no voice in it: I'll
          make my old clothes know who's master. I shall straightway
          cashier the hunting-frock, and render my leather breeches
          incapable. My hair has been in training some time.

ABSOLUTE. Indeed!

ACRES.   Ay—and tho'ff the side curls are a little restive, my hind-
          part takes it very kindly.

ABSOLUTE. Oh, you'll polish, I doubt not.

ACRES.   Absolutely I propose so—then if I can find out this Ensign
          Beverley, odds triggers and flints! I'll make him know the
          difference o't.

ABSOLUTE. Spoke like a man! But pray, Bob, I observe you have got
          an odd kind of a new method of swearing—

ACRES.   Ha! ha! you've taken notice of it—'tis genteel, isn't it!—I
          didn't invent it myself though, but a commander in our
          militia, a great scholar, I assure you, says that there is no
          meaning in the common oaths, and that nothing but their
          antiquity makes them respectable; because, he says, the
          ancients would never stick to an oath or two, but would say,
          by Jove! or by Bacchus! or by Mars! or by Venus! or by
          Pallas, according to the sentiment: so that to swear with
          propriety, says my little major, the oath should be an echo
          to the sense; and this we call the *oath referential*, or *sentimen-
          tal swearing*—ha! ha! 'tis genteel, isn't it.

ABSOLUTE. Very genteel, and very new, indeed!—and I dare say will
          supplant all other figures of imprecation.

ACRES.   Ay, ay, the best terms will grow obsolete.—Damns have
          had their day.

The Duenna

The Duenna, *again by Sheridan, was first performed in
1775. This song from the play constitutes a charming comment
on the eighteenth-century equivalent of computer-dating.*

Ah! sure a pair was never seen
    So justly form'd to meet by nature!
The youth excelling so in mien,
      The maid in ev'ry grace of feature.
        Oh, how happy are such lovers,
          When kindred beauties each discovers:
            For surely she
            Was made for thee,
      And thou to bless this lovely creature!

So mild your looks, your children thence
    Will early learn the task of duty—
Thy boys with all their father's sense,
      The girls with all their mother's beauty!
        Oh, how happy to inherit
          At once such graces and such spirit!
           Thus while you live
           May fortune give
      Each blessing equal to your merit!

The School for Scandal

This rather charming drinking song appears in
The School for Scandal *by Sheridan, staged in 1777.*

Here's to the maiden of bashful fifteen;
    Here's to the widow of fifty;
Here's to the flaunting extravagant quean,
    And here's to the housewife that's thrifty.
Chorus:
    Let the toast pass,—
    Drink to the lass,
I'll warrant she'll prove an excuse for a glass.

Here's to the charmer whose dimples we prize;
    Now to the maid who had none, sir;
Here's to the girl with a pair of blue eyes,
    And here's to the nymph with but one, sir.
Chorus:
    Let the toast pass,—
    Drink to the lass,
I'll warrant she'll prove an excuse for a glass.

Here's to the maid with a bosom of snow:
    Now to her that's as brown as a berry:
Here's to the wife with a face full of woe,
    And now to the damsel that's merry.
Chorus:
    Let the toast pass,—
    Drink to the lass,
I'll warrant she'll prove an excuse for a glass.

For let 'em be clumsy, or let 'em be slim,
    Young or ancient, I care not a feather;
So fill a pint bumper quite up to the brim,
So fill up your glasses, nay, fill to the brim,
    And let us e'en toast them together.
Chorus:
    Let the toast pass,—
    Drink to the lass,
I'll warrant she'll prove an excuse for a glass.

To Julia

*This is one of the 'Little Poems' of Thomas Moore, compiler of
the famous* Moore's Irish Melodies, *published in 1802. He is
credited with being a great writer of bawdy verse.
Unfortunately, I have been unable to find any examples.*

Well, Julia, if to love, and live
'Mid all the pleasures love can give,
    Be crimes that bring damnation;
You—you and I have giv'n such scope
To loves and joys, we scarce can hope,
    In heav'n, the least salvation!

And yet, I think, did Heav'n design
That blisses dear, like yours and mine,
    Should be our own undoing;
It had not made my soul so warm,
Nor giv'n you such a witching form,
    To bid me dote on ruin!

Then wipe away that timid tear;
Sweet truant! you have nought to fear,
    Though you were whelm'd in sin;
Stand but at heaven's gate awhile,
And you *so like an angel* smile,
    They can't but *let you in.*

To Phillis

This is another example of Moore's 'Little Poems'; together with the one above and the one below it gives credence to the last of these 'Little Poems'.

Phillis, you little rosy rake,
    That heart of yours I long to rifle;
Come, give it me, and do not make
    So much ado about a *trifle!*

The Kiss

The wry humour of this piece constitutes a great deal of its charm.

Give me, my love, that billing kiss,
    I taught you one delicious night,
When, turning epicures in bliss,
    We tried inventions of delight.

Come, gently steal my lips along,
    And let your lips in murmurs move.—
Ah! no—again—that kiss was wrong,—
    How can you be so dull, my love?

'Cease, cease!' the blushing girl replied,
    And in her milky arms she caught me—
'How can you thus your pupil chide?
    'You know *'t was in the dark* you taught me!'

The Catalogue

*The absence of both Julia and Phillis from this final 'Little Poem'
leads one to believe that the poet has not been totally honest!*

'Come, tell me,' says Rosa, as kissing and kist,
　　One day she reclin'd on my breast;
'Come tell me the number, repeat me the list
　　'Of the nymphs you have lov'd and carest.'
Oh Rosa! 't was only my fancy that rov'd,
　　My heart at the moment was free;
But I'll tell you, my girl, how many I've lov'd,
　　And the number shall finish with thee!

My tutor was Kitty: in infancy wild
　　She taught me the way to be blest;
She taught me to love her—I lov'd like a child,
　　But Kitty could fancy the rest.
This lesson of dear and enrapturing lore
　　I have never forgot, I allow;
I have had it *by rote* very often before,
　　But never *by heart* until now!

Pretty Martha was next, and my soul was all flame,
　　But my head was so full of romance,
That I fancied her into some chivalry dame,
　　And I was her knight of the lance!
But Martha was not of this fanciful school,
　　And she'd laugh at her poor little knight;
While I thought her a goddess, she thought me a fool,
　　And I'll swear, *she* was most in the right.

My soul was now calm, till by Cloris's looks
　　Again I was tempted to rove;
But Cloris, I found, was so learned in books,
　　That she gave me more logic than love!

So I left this young Sappho, and hasten'd to fly
　　To those sweeter logicians in bliss,
Who argue the point with a soul-telling eye,
　　And convince us at once with a kiss!

Oh! Susan was then all the world unto me,
　　But Susan was piously given;
And the worst of it was, we could never agree
　　On the road that was shortest to heaven!
Oh Susan! I've said, in the moments of mirth,
　　What's devotion to thee or to me?
I devoutly believe there's a heaven on earth,
　　And believe that *that* heaven's in *thee*!

Believe Me, If All Those Endearing Young Charms

It would be impossible not to include one at least of the 'Irish Melodies' for which Thomas Moore was famous—despite the fact that for a time it was fashionable to sneer at him.

Believe me, if all those endearing young charms,
　　Which I gaze on so fondly today,
Were to change by to-morrow, and fleet in my arms,
　　Like fairy-gifts fading away!
Thou wouldst still be adored, as this moment thou art,
　　Let thy loveliness fade as it will,
And around the dear ruin, each wish of my heart
　　Would entwine itself verdantly still!

It is not while beauty and youth are thine own,
　　And thy cheeks unprofaned by a tear,
That the fervour and faith of a soul can be known,
　　To which time will but make thee more dear!

121

Oh! the heart that has truly loved never forgets
    But as truly loves on to the close,
As the sun flower turns on her god, when she sets,
    The same look which she turned when he rose!

Mantle So Green

*This is a street ballad that presumably was composed shortly
after Napoleon's defeat at Waterloo in 1815.*

As I walked out one morning in June,
To view the fair fields and meadows green,
I spied a young damsel she appeared like a queen,
With her costly fine robes and her mantle so green.

I stood in amazement and struck with surprise,
I thought her an angel that fell from the skies.
Her eyes like the diamond her cheeks like the rose
She is one of the fairest that nature composed.

Said I pretty fair maid if you come with me,
We will join in wedlock and married we'll be,
I'll dress you in rich attire you'll appear like a queen
With your costly fine robes and your mantle so green.

She answered me young man you must be refused
For I'll wed with no man you must me excuse,
To the green hills I'll wander to shun all men's view
For the lad that I love lies in famed Waterloo.

Since you are not married tell me your lover's name
I have been in battle I might know the same,
Draw to my garment and there you will see,
His name is embroidered on my mantle so green.

On the raising of her mantle it's there I beheld,
His name and his surname in letters of gold,
Young William O'Reilly appeared in my view,
'He was my chief comrade in famed Waterloo.'

'We fought so victorious where bullets did fly,
And in the field of Norvan your true lover does lie
We fought for three days to the fourth afternoon,
He received his death summons on the eighteenth of June.'

'When he was dying I heard his last cry,
Were you here lovely Nancy in peace I would die
Peace is proclaimed and truth I declare,
There is your love's token the gold ring I wear.'

She stood in amazement the paler she grew,
She flew from my arms with her heart full of woe,
To the green hills I'll wander for the lad that I love
Rise up lovely Nancy your grief I'll remove.

Oh, Nancy lovely Nancy it was I won your heart,
In your father's garden that day we did part,
In your father's garden within a green shadow tree
Where I rolled in your arms in your mantle so green.

These couple got married I heard people say,
Great Nobles attended their wedding, that day
Peace is proclaimed and the war is all over,
You're welcome to my arms lovely Nancy once more.

A Love Song to My Wife

This refreshing tribute to a living wife is by Joseph Brennan.

Come to me, darling one, nearer and nearer—
Time only renders you dearer and dearer.
Grief has no chill for the love which is truthful;
Years, as they roll, find it brilliantly youthful—
Steadfastly scorning a moment of ranging—
Changes around find affection unchanging.
Brightly it silvers the clouds which are o'er us:
Nightly it lights up the pathway before us.

See you that calm and majestical river,
Stealing on tranquilly, ever and ever—
Beautiful always, in sunshine or shadow,
Breasting the tempest, or kissing the meadow—
Bountiful, too, in its musical flowing—
Source of the green which beside it is glowing;
Soul of the woods which so verdantly bound it;
Seed of the flowers which are laughing around it?

Dear! as that river flows onward and onward,
Forcing the seeds of fertility sunward;
So has the current of love for you glided,
Bright'ning the years which are gathered beside it—
Clothing their forms with a raiment of purple;
Gracing their heads with the laurel and myrtle;
Making each hour, which in quiet reposes,
Break into beauty and blush into roses.

Surely that stream has a lesson for lovers:
O'er it a silver-clad sisterhood hovers—
Birds which, illuming the proximate grasses,
Peck into dimples the wave as it passes—
Birds which fulfill their predestinate duty,
Lending their hues to completion of beauty,
Bright in the nooning or dark in the even,
Ultimate tints in the landscape of heaven!

Thus, as our love hurries on to its ending,
Beautiful things with its beauties are blending;—
Fancies which nest in the years by it, dreaming
Silver-clad thoughts which are constantly gleaming;
Gifts which, at evening, the shadow enhances,
Breaking to joys as the morning advances;
Hope for the future, and fond recollection—
Golden-hued guardian of human affection.

But, if some casual wing of ill-omen
Glides o'er the wave like the shade of the gnomon;—
What if the song-birds at times have been wearied;
What if the sunshine has not been unvaried;
What if the buds of our spring which departed
Left us in solitude weak and sad-hearted;
What if we sometimes have moments of weeping
Over the little ones death has set sleeping?

Let them sleep on: there are dreams in their slumbers,
Soothed by the angels' most musical numbers;
Lit by the light of a greatness supernal;
Blest by the bliss which alone is eternal.
Let them sleep on: they are happy above us,
Death cannot make them unable to love us;—
Weep not for babes which are benisons o'er us;
Grieve not because they are happy before us!

Come to me, darling one, nearer and nearer,
Time only renders you dearer and dearer.
Grief has no chill for the love which is truthful;
Years, as they roll, find it brilliantly youthful—
Steadfastly scorning a moment of ranging—
Changes around leave affection unchanging.
Brightly it silvers the clouds which are o'er us:
Nightly it lights up the pathway before us!

I'd Swear for Her

*This amusing declaration of, literally, undying love is
attributed to James Doherty.*

I'd swear for her,
I'd tear for her,
The Lord knows what I'd bear for her;
I'd lie for her,
I'd sigh for her,
I'd drink Lough Erne dry for her;
I'd 'cuss' for her,
Do 'muss' for her,
I'd kick up a thundering fuss for her;
I'd weep for her,
I'd leap for her,
I'd go without any sleep for her;
I'd fight for her,
I'd bite for her,
I'd walk the streets all night for her;
I'd plead for her,
I'd bleed for her,
I'd go without my 'feed' for her;
I'd shoot for her,
I'd boot for her
A rival who'd come to 'suit' for her;

I'd kneel for her,
I'd steal for her,
Such is the love I feel for her;
I'd slide for her,
I'd ride for her,
I'd swim against wind and tide for her;
I'd try for her,
I'd cry for her,
But—hang me if I'd die for her
Or any other woman!

And Then No More

*This is a pleasing example of the original work in English of the
early nineteenth-century poet James Clarence Mangan.*

I saw her once, one little while, and then no more:
'Twas Eden's light on Earth awhile, and then no more.
Amid the throng she passed along the meadow-floor:
Spring seemed to smile on Earth awhile, and then no more;
But whence she came, which way she went, what garb she wore
I noted not; I gazed awhile, and then no more!

I saw her once, one little while, and then no more:
'Twas Paradise on Earth awhile, and then no more.
Ah! what avail my vigils pale, my magic lore?
She shone before mine eyes awhile, and then no more.
The shallop of my peace is wrecked on Beauty's shore.
Near Hope's fair isle it rode awhile, and then no more!

I saw her once, one little while, and then no more:
The earth was Peri-land awhile, and then no more.
Oh, might I see but once again, as once before,
Through chance or wile, that shape awhile, and then no more!
Death soon would heal my griefs! This heart, now sad and sore,
Would beat anew a little while, and then no more.

A White Rose

A charming example of the work of the little-known mid-nineteenth-century poet John Boyle O'Reilly.

The red rose whispers of passion,
And the white rose breathes of love;
O, the red rose is a falcon,
And the white rose is a dove.

But I send you a cream-white rosebud,
With a flush on its petal tips;
For the love that is purest and sweetest
Has a kiss of desire on the lips.

To the Beloved

Whether or not Liain actually wrote the ninth-century poem ascribed to her (p. 48), apart from Eibhlín Dhubh Ní Chonaill, female authors are not frequently encountered in Irish literature, in English or Irish, until relatively recent times. This poem by Alice Furlong, from her Roses and Rue, *published in 1899, is an example of a poem by a respected female poet of the late nineteenth century.*

Love of you and hate of you
Tears my very heart in two!
As you please me or displease,
So I burn and so I freeze.

I would build your wattled dun
With a gold roof like the sun;
I would stain the trellis bars
With the silver of the stars.

At my bitter heart's behoof
I would wreck your radiant roof;
Of your twinkling trellises
All my anger jealous is.

I would give you great-horned rams,
Mild-eyed sheep, and milk-white lambs,
Fit for any king to own,
By the turning of the stone.

I would set your rams astray,
I would wile your sheep away,
With their lambs' milk-white exceeding,
For the grey wolf's famished feeding.

I would guide the oxen meek,
And the ploughshare's silver beak
O'er your land to make it meet
For the sowing of the wheat.

I would blight your team with blain,
I would rust your ploughs with rain,
In your furrows, deep and brown,
I would scatter thistle-down.

I would put twelve milking cows
On your pastures green to browse;
I would set twelve tubs of cream
On your dairy's oaken beam.

Blasted by a curse of mine,
All your cows should ail and pine;
From your fields I'd skim the dew—
Steal the cream away from you.

Under your grey apple trees
I would hive the honey bees;
Store away in each gold dome
Lush, delicious honey-comb.

From the boughs of rose and grey
I would charm the bees away,
Bitter bread might be your share
On the days of Easter fare.

I would crown your head with gold,
Robe you fine in silken fold,
Win for you a magic wand
From Danaan fairy-land.

I would break your golden crown,
I would rend your silken gown,
I would burn your magic wand
From Danaan fairy-land.

I would place you on a throne,
I would give you all to own,
All of me and all of mine:
I would make you half-divine.

I would leave you in sore want,
I would have you hunger-gaunt,
I would bring you to my feet
In subjection most complete.

I would lift you to the skies,
I would give you paradise;
I would suffer hell's worst dole
For the saving of your soul.

Wounding coldness to reprove
I would wound you in my love.
Suppliant still at your heart's gate
I do worship in my hate.

Requiescat

While Oscar Wilde is best known for his witty plays, he could also write very delicately.

Tread lightly, she is near
    Under the snow,
Speak gently, she can hear
    The daisies grow.

All her bright golden hair
    Tarnished with rust,
She that was young and fair
    Fallen to dust.

Lily-like, white as snow,
    She hardly knew
She was a woman, so
    Sweetly she grew.

Coffin-board, heavy stone,
    Lie on her breast,
I vex my heart alone,
    She is at rest.

Peace, Peace, she cannot hear
    Lyre or sonnet,
All my life's buried here,
    Heap earth upon it.

Dread

*J. M. Synge, like Oscar Wilde, was best known for his plays;
he also wrote poetry.*

Beside a chapel I'd a room looked down,
Where all the women from the farms and town,
On holy days, and Sundays used to pass
To marriages, and christenings and to Mass.

Then I sat lonely watching score and score,
Till I turned jealous of the Lord next door ...
Now by this window, where there's none can see,
The Lord God's jealous of yourself and me.

A Question

*Another example—rather poignant—of the poetic
work of J. M. Synge.*

I asked if I got sick and died, would you
With my black funeral go walking too,
If you'd stand close to hear them talk or pray
While I'm let down in that steep bank of clay.

And, No, you said, for if you saw a crew
Of living idiots, pressing round that new
Oak coffin—they alive, I dead beneath
That board—you'd rave and rend them with your teeth.

Letter to Molly

*One of the gentle love-letters of J. M. Synge to his beloved Molly
Allgood, from whom, she being an actress with the Abbey
Theatre, he was often separated.*

My thousand Treasures

I opened your letter this morning with terror—I knew I deserved
a scolding and I was afraid I was going to 'catch it'. You let me off
very well and I am in wild good spirits now. Dear Heart in four
Days—damn them—I will be in the Seventh Heaven again, with my
little changeling, my little jewel, my love and life, in my arms! Is not
that something to live for. Dearest if you could see how I get up
thinking of my little changeling, and go to bed thinking about my little changeling, about her little baby nose, and her little eyes, and her
little voice, and her little bull-dog chin, and all her little soul and
body that is mine forever!

Dear Heart, Dear Heart, Dear Heart if you knew how much you
are to me! How I see you waiting for me at the door of the scenery
room, and sitting on my knee among the quiet woods, and putting a
new life into the stars and streams and trees and Heaven and Earth
and all that therein is for me! I had better stop I think or I might blas-
pheme God in my love for you.

I send some lines I scratched off last night if they make you smile
remember they are a first draft only. I send also a foolish letter I wrote
last night. Now for the Play Boy—God confound him!

Goodbye my own dearest Heart.

Your Tramp.

Many thanks for all your news. It interested me greatly. I fear you are
right about Yeats' plays. Good bye again, my single darling love, my
treasure of life.

A Mayo Love Song

Alice Milligan was a distinguished translator of poetry from the Irish. This one is from her Hero Lays, *published in 1908.*

It is far, and it is far,
To Connemara where you are,
To where its purple glens enfold you
As glooming heavens that hold a star.

But they shall shine, they yet shall shine,
Colleen, those eyes of yours on mine
Like stars that after eve assemble,
And tremble over the mountain line.

Though it be far, though it be far,
I'll journey over to where you are,
By grasslands green that lie between
And shining lakes at Mullingar.

And we shall be, and we shall be,
Oh, Colleen lonely, beloved by me,
For evermore on a moor of Mayo
'Mid heather singing like the sea.

Deirdre

This extract from the play Deirdre *by W. B. Yeats, based on the early romantic tale of the exile of the sons of Uisneach, written in 1907, is a very moving dramatisation of the last encounter of the two lovers in front of Conchubar. It is by no means a translation of anything in the original Irish version.*

[*Conchubar enters with dark-faced men.*]

CONCHUBAR. One woman and two men; that is the quarrel
    That knows no mending. Bring in the man she chose
    Because of his beauty and the strength of his youth.
    [*The dark-faced men drag in Naoise entangled in a net.*]

NAOISE. I have been taken like a bird or a fish.

CONCHUBAR. He cried 'Beast, beast!' and in a blind-beast rage
    He ran at me and fell into the nets,
    But we were careful for your sake, and took him
    With all the comeliness that woke desire
    Unbroken in him. I being old and lenient,
    I would not hurt a hair upon his head.

DEIRDRE. What do you say? Have you forgiven him?

NAOISE. He is but mocking us. What's left to say
    Now that the seven years' hunt is at an end?

DEIRDRE. He never doubted you until I made him,
    And therefore all the blame for what he says
    Should fall on me.

CONCHUBAR. But his young blood is hot,
    And if we're of one mind, he shall go free,
    And I ask nothing for it, or, if something,
    Nothing I could not take. There is no king
    In the wide world that, being so greatly wronged,
    Could copy me, and give all vengeance up.
    Although her marriage-day had all but come,

You carried her away; but I'll show mercy.
Because you had the insolent strength of youth
You carried her away; but I've had time
To think it out through all these seven years.
I will show mercy.

NAOISE. You have many words.

CONCHUBAR. I will not make a bargain; but I ask
What is already mine.

[*Deirdre moves slowly towards Conchubar while he is speaking,
her eyes fixed upon him.*]

                    You may go free
If Deirdre will but walk into my house
Before the people's eyes, that they may know,
When I have put the crown upon her head,
I have not taken her by force and guile.
The doors are open, and the floors are strewed
And in the bridal chamber curtains sewn
With all enchantments that give happiness
By races that are germane to the sun,
And nearest him, and have no blood in their veins—
For when they're wounded the wound drips with wine—
Nor speech but singing. At the bridal door
Two fair king's daughters carry in their hands
The crown and robe.

DEIRDRE.   O no! Not that, not that!
Ask any other thing but that one thing.
Leave me with Naoise. We will go away
Into some country at the ends of the earth.
We'll trouble you no more; and there is no one
That will not praise you if you pardon us.
'He is good, he is good', they'll say to one another:
'There's nobody like him, for he forgave
Deirdre and Naoise.'

CONCHUBAR.   Do you think that I
Shall let you go again, after seven years
Of longing and of planning here and there,
And trafficking with merchants for the stones

That make all sure, and watching my own face
That none might read it?

DEIRDRE [*to Naoise*].   It's better to go with him.
Why should you die when one can bear it all?
My life is over; it's better to obey.
Why should you die? I will not live long, Naoise.
I'd not have you believe I'd long stay living;
O no, no, no! You will go far away.
You will forget me. Speak, speak, Naoise, speak,
And say that it is better that I go.
I will not ask it. Do not speak a word,
For I will take it all upon myself.
Conchubar, I will go.

NAOISE.   And do you think
That, were I given life at such a price,
I would not cast it from me? O my eagle!
Why do you beat vain wings upon the rock
When hollow night's above?

DEIRDRE.   It's better, Naoise.
It may be hard for you, but you'll forget.
For what am I, to be remembered always?
And there are other women. There was one,
The daughter of the King of Leodas;
I could not sleep because of her. Speak to him;
Tell it out plain, and make him understand.
And if it be he thinks I shall stay living,
Say that I will not.

NAOISE.   Would I had lost life
Among those Scottish kings that sought it of me
Because you were my wife, or that the worst
Had taken you before this bargaining!
O eagle! If you were to do this thing,
And buy my life of Conchubar with your body,
Love's law being broken, I would stand alone
Upon the eternal summits, and call out,
And you could never come there, being banished.

DEIRDRE [*kneeling to Conchubar*]. I would obey, but cannot.
    Pardon us.
    I know that you are good. I have heard you praised
    For giving gifts; and you will pardon us,
    Although I cannot go into your house.
    It was my fault. I only should be punished.
    [*Unseen by Deirdre, Naoise is gagged.*]
    The very moment these eyes fell on him,
    I told him; I held out my hands to him;
    How could he refuse? At first he would not—
    I am not lying—he remembered you.
    What do I say? My hands?—No, no, my lips—
    For I had pressed my lips upon his lips—
    I swear it is not false—my breast to his;
    [*Conchubar motions; Naoise, unseen by Deirdre, is taken behind the curtain.*]
    Until I woke the passion that's in all,
    And how could he resist? I had my beauty.
    You may have need of him, a brave, strong man,
    Who is not foolish at the council-board,
    Nor does he quarrel by the candle-light
    And give hard blows to dogs. A cup of wine
    Moves him to mirth, not madness.
    [*She stands up.*]
                      What am I saying?
    You may have need of him, for you have none
    Who is so good a sword, or so well loved
    Among the common people. You may need him,
    And what king knows when the hour of need may come?
    You dream that you have men enough. You laugh.
    Yes; you are laughing to yourself. You say,
    'I am Conchubar—I have no need of him.'
    You will cry out for him some day and say,
    'If Naoise were but living'—
    [*She misses Naoise*]   Where is he?
    Where have you sent him? Where is the son of Usna?
    Where is he, O, where is he?

[*She staggers over to the Musicians. The Executioner has come out with a sword on which there is blood; Conchubar points to it. The Musicians give a wail.*]

CONCHUBAR. The traitor who has carried off my wife
     No longer lives. Come to my house now, Deirdre,
     For he that called himself your husband's dead.

DEIRDRE. O, Do not touch me. Let me go to him.
     [*Pause*]
     King Conchubar is right. My husband's dead.
     A single woman is of no account,
     Lacking array of servants, linen cupboards,
     The bacon hanging—and King Conchubar's house
     All ready, too—I'll to King Conchubar's house.
     It is but wisdom to do willingly
     What has to be.

CONCHUBAR.   But why are you so calm?
     I thought that you would curse me and cry out,
     And fall upon the ground and tear your hair.

DEIRDRE [*laughing*]. You know too much of women to think so;
     Though, if I were less worthy of desire,
     I would pretend as much; but, being myself,
     It is enough that you were master here.
     Although we are so delicately made,
     There's something brutal in us, and we are won
     By those who can shed blood. It was some woman
     That taught you how to woo: but do not touch me;
     I shall do all you bid me, but not yet,
     Because I have to do what's customary.
     We lay the dead out, folding up the hands,
     Closing the eyes, and stretching out the feet,
     And push a pillow underneath the head,
     Till all's in order; and all this I'll do
     For Naoise, son of Usna.

CONCHUBAR.   It is not fitting.
     You are not now a wanderer, but a queen,
     And there are plenty that can do these things.

DEIRDRE [*motioning Conchubar away*]. No, no. Not yet. I cannot be
      your queen
      Till the past's finished, and its debts are paid.
      When a man dies, and there are debts unpaid,
      He wanders by the debtor's bed and cries,
      'There's so much owing.'

CONCHUBAR.   You are deceiving me.
      You long to look upon his face again.
      Why should I give you now to a dead man
      That took you from a living?
      [*He makes a step towards her.*]

DEIRDRE.   In good time.
      You'll stir me to more passion than he could,
      And yet, if you are wise, you'll grant me this:
      That I go look upon him that was once
      So strong and comely and held his head so high
      That women envied me. For I will see him
      All blood-bedabbled and his beauty gone.
      It's better, when you're beside me in your strength,
      That the mind's eye should call up the soiled body,
      And not the shape I loved. Look at him, women.
      He heard me pleading to be given up,
      Although my lover was still living, and yet
      He doubts my purpose. I will have you tell him
      How changeable all women are; how soon
      Even the best of lovers is forgot
      When his day's finished.

CONCHUBAR.   No; but I will trust
      The strength that you have praised, and not your purpose.

DEIRDRE [*almost with a caress*]. It is so small a gift and you will grant it
      Because it is the first that I have asked.
      He has refused. There is no sap in him;
      Nothing but empty veins. I thought as much.
      He has refused me the first thing I have asked—
      Me, me, his wife. I understand him now;
      I know the sort of life I'll have with him;
      But he must drag me to his house by force.

If he refuses [*she laughs*], he shall be mocked of all.
They'll say to one another, 'Look at him
That is so jealous that he lured a man
From over sea, and murdered him, and yet
He trembled at the thought of a dead face!'
[*She has her hand upon curtain.*]

CONCHUBAR. How do I know that you have not some knife,
    And go to die upon his body?

DEIRDRE.   Have me searched,
    If you would make so little of your queen.
    It may be that I have a knife hid here
    Under my dress. Bid one of these dark slaves
    To search me for it.
    [*Pause.*]

CONCHUBAR.   Go to your farewells, Queen.

He Wishes for the Cloths of Heaven

Much of the lyric poetry of W. B. Yeats between 1888 and 1901
was inspired by his love for Maud Gonne. There is a strong note
of realism in the line 'But I, being poor ...'

Had I the heavens' embroidered cloths,
Enwrought with golden and silver light,
The blue and the dim and the dark cloths
Of night and light and the half-light,
I would spread the cloths under your feet:
But I, being poor, have only my dreams;
I have spread my dreams under your feet;
Tread softly because you tread on my dreams.

First Love

Although this was written in 1926 or 1927, after the
marriage of Maud Gonne, it is still strongly influenced by
Yeats's love for her.

Though nurtured like the sailing moon
In beauty's murderous brood,
She walked awhile and blushed awhile
And on my pathway stood
Until I thought her body bore
A heart of flesh and blood.

But since I laid a hand thereon
And found a heart of stone
I have attempted many things
And not a thing is done,
For every hand is lunatic
That travels on the moon.

She smiled and that transfigured me
And left me but a lout,
Maundering here, and maundering there,
Emptier of thought
Than the heavenly circuit of its stars
When the moon sails out.

Affinity

This poem, from the collected works of George Russell (better known, perhaps, by his cypher 'Æ'), published in 1915, shows a delicate, almost oblique, approach to love.

You and I have found the secret way,
None can bar our love or say us nay:
All the world may stare and never know
You and I are twined together so.

You and I for all his vaunted width
Know the giant Space is but a myth;
Over miles and miles of pure deceit
You and I have found our lips can meet.

You and I have laughed the leagues apart
In the soft delight of heart to heart.
If there's a gulf to meet or limit set,
You and I have never found it yet.

You and I have trod the backward way
To the happy heart of yesterday,
To the love we felt in ages past.
You and I have found it still to last.

You and I have found the joy had birth
In the angel childhood of the earth,
Hid within the heart of man and maid.
You and I of Time are not afraid.

A Call

Again by George Russell, this poem shows the almost inevitable remembrance of things from a Celtic past of the Irish, writing in English, at this period.

Dusk its ash-grey blossoms sheds on violet skies,
Over twilight mountains where the heart songs rise,
Rise and fall and fade away from earth to air.
Earth renews the music sweeter. Oh, come there.
Come, acushla, come, as in ancient times
Rings aloud the underland with faery chimes.
Down the unseen ways as strays each tinkling fleece
Winding ever onward to a fold of peace,
So my dreams go straying in a land more fair;
Half I tread the dew-wet grasses, half wander there.
Fade your glimmering eyes in a world grown cold;
Come, acushla, with me to the mountains old.
There the bright ones call us waving to and fro—
Come my children, with me to the ancient go.

Heroic Love

The awareness of a heroic past is even more explicit in this poem, also by George Russell.

When our glowing dreams were dead,
Ruined our heroic piles,
Something in your dark eyes said:
'Think no more of love or smiles.'

Something in me still would say,
'Though our dreamland palace goes,
I have seen how in decay
Still the wild rose clings and blows.'

But your dark eyes willed it thus:
'Build our lofty dream again:
Let our palace rise o'er us:
Love can never be till then.'

Desire

*This, the last of the George Russell poems to be given, could as
easily be construed as an expression of the love of God as the
love of a person.*

With Thee a moment! Then what dreams have play!
Traditions of eternal toil arise,
Search for the high, austere and lonely way
The Spirit moves in through eternities.
Ah, in the soul what memories arise!

And with what yearning inexpressible,
Rising from long forgetfulness I turn
To Thee, invisible, unrumoured, still:
White for Thy whiteness all desires burn.
Ah, with what longing once again I turn!

To the Beloved

*By the twentieth century the work of female authors was much
more readily available in print. A well-known author of the
earlier part of the century was Katharine Tynan. This piece is
from her series 'Songs of Love, Life and Death' from her*
Collected Poems, *published in 1930.*

You were a part of the green country,
    Of the grey hills and the quiet places;
They are not the same, the fields and the mountains,
    Without the lost and beloved faces,
And you were a part of the sweet country.

There's a road that winds by the foot of the mountains
    Where I run in my dreams and you come to meet me,
With your blue eyes and your cheeks' old roses,
    The old fond smile that was quick to greet me.
They are not the same, the fields and the mountains.

There is something lost, there is something lonely,
    The birds are singing, the streams are calling,
The sun's the same, and the wind in the meadows.
    But o'er your grave are the shadows falling,
The soul is missing, and all is lonely.

It is what they said: you were part of the country,
    You were never afraid of the wind and weather,
I can hear in dreams the feet of your pony,
    You and your pony coming together,
You will drive no more through the pleasant country.

You were part of the fields and mountains,
    Everyone knew you, everyone loved you;
All the world was your friend and neighbour,
    The women smiled and the men approved you.
They are not the same, the fields and the mountains.

I sigh no more for the pleasant places,
    The longer I've lost you the more I miss you.
My heart seeks you in dreams and shadows,
    In dreams I find you, in dreams I kiss you,
And wake, alas! to the lonely places.

When the Ecstatic Body Grips

*Eric Dodds, a distinguished classicist and a professor at
Oxford, is probably not very well known as a
twentieth-century Irish poet.*

When the ecstatic body grips
Its heaven, with little sobbing cries,
And lips are crushed on hot blind lips,
I read strange pity in your eyes.

For that in you which is not mine,
And that in you which I love best,
And that, which my day-thoughts divine
Masterless still, still unpossessed,

Sits in the blue eyes' frightened stare,
A naked lonely-dwelling thing,
A frail thing from its body-lair
Drawn at my body's summoning;

Whispering low, 'O unknown man,
Whose hunger on my hunger wrought,
Body shall give what body can,
Shall give you all—save what you sought.'

Whispering, 'O secret one, forgive,
Forgive and be content though still
Beyond the blood's surrender live
The darkness of the separate will.

'Enough if in the veins we know
Body's delirium, body's peace—
Ask not that ghost to ghost shall go,
Essence in essence merge and cease.'

But swiftly, as in sudden sleep,
That You in you is veiled or dead;
And the world's shrunken to a heap
Of hot flesh straining on a bed.

I Would Like
My Love to Die

Samuel Beckett too is much better known as a playwright
than as a poet.

I would like my love to die
and the rain to be raining on the graveyard
and on me walking the streets
mourning her who thought she loved me.

She Moved Through the Fair

This song, or poem, is so well known and so commonly assumed to be an ancient and traditional piece that it is almost impossible to believe that it is actually the work of Pádraic Colum, who died as recently as 1972.

My young love said to me, 'My brothers won't mind,
And my parents won't slight you for your lack of kind.'
Then she stepped away from me, and this she did say,
'It will not be long, love, till our wedding day.'

She stepped away from me and she moved through the fair,
And fondly I watched her go here and go there,
Then she went her way homeward with one star awake,
As the swan in the evening moves over the lake.

The people were saying no two were e'er wed
But one had a sorrow that never was said,
And I smiled as she passed with her goods and her gear,
And that was the last that I saw of my dear.

I dreamt it last night that my young love came in,
So softly she entered, her feet made no din;
She came close beside me, and this she did say,
'It will not be long, love, till our wedding day.'

Autumn Journal

*This extract is from Louis MacNeice's chattily powerful long
poem Autumn Journal, written in 1939. MacNeice was a very
human and contemporary poet.*

September has come and I wake
    And I think with joy how whatever, now or in future, the system
Nothing whatever can take
    The people away, there will always be people
For friends or for lovers though perhaps
    The conditions of love will be changed and its vices diminished
And affection not lapse
    To narrow possessiveness, jealousy founded on vanity.
September has come, it is *hers*
    Whose vitality leaps in the autumn,
Whose nature prefers
    Trees without leaves and a fire in the fire-place;
So I give her this month and the next
    Though the whole of my year should be hers who has rendered
    already
So many of its days intolerable or perplexed
    But so many more so happy;
Who has left a scent on my life and left my walls
    Dancing over and over with her shadow,
Whose hair is twined in all my waterfalls
    And all of London littered with remembered kisses.
So I am glad
    That life contains her with her moods and moments
More shifting and more transient than I had
    Yet thought of as being integral to beauty;
Whose mind is like the wind on a sea of wheat,
    Whose eyes are candour,

And assurance in her feet
>Like a homing pigeon never by doubt diverted.

To whom I send my thanks
>That the air has become shot silk, the streets are music,

And that the ranks
>Of men are ranks of men, no more of cyphers.

So that if now alone
>I must pursue this life, it will not be only

A drag from numbered stone to numbered stone
>But a ladder of angels, river turning tidal.

Offhand, at times hysterical, abrupt,
>*You* are one I always shall remember,

Whom cant can never corrupt
>Nor argument disinherit.

Frivolous, always in a hurry, forgetting the address,
>Frowning too often, taking enormous notice

Of hats and backchat—how could I assess
>The thing that makes you different?

You whom I remember glad or tired,
>Smiling in drink or scintillating anger,

Inopportunely desired
>On boats, on trains, on roads when walking.

Sometimes untidy, often elegant,
>So easily hurt, so readily responsive,

To whom a trifle could be an irritant
>Or could be balm and manna.

Whose words would tumble over each other and pelt
>From pure excitement,

Whose fingers curl and melt
>When you were friendly.

I shall remember you in bed with bright
>Eyes or in a café stirring coffee

Abstractedly and on your plate the white
>Smoking stub your lips had touched with crimson.

And I shall remember how your words could hurt
>Because they were so honest

And even your lies were able to assert
    Integrity of purpose.
And it is on the strength of knowing you
    I reckon generous feeling more important
Than the mere deliberating what to do
    When neither the pros nor cons affect the pulses.
And though I have suffered from your special strength
    Who never flatter for points nor fake responses,
I should be proud if I could evolve at length
An equal thrust and pattern.

Trilogy for X

These two portions of the trilogy by Louis MacNeice
demonstrate amusingly different attitudes to love and sex.

I

When clerks and navvies fondle
    Beside canals their wenches,
In rapture or in coma
    The haunches that they handle,
And the orange moon sits idle
    Above the orchard slanted—
Upon such easy evenings
    We take our loves for granted.

But when, as now, the creaking
    Trees on the hills of London
Like bison charge their neighbours
    In wind that keeps us waking
And in the draught the scolloped
    Lampshade swings a shadow,
We think of love bound over—
    The mortgage on the meadow.

And one lies lonely, haunted
    By limbs he half remembers,
And one, in wedlock, wonders
    Where is the girl he wanted;
And some sit smoking, flicking
    The ash away and feeling
For love gone up like vapour
    Between the floor and ceiling.

But now when winds are curling
    The trees do you come closer,
Close as an eyelid fasten
    My body in darkness, darling;
Switch the light off and let me
    Gather you up and gather
The power of trains advancing
    Further, advancing further.

II

And love hung still as crystal over the bed
    And filled the corners of the enormous room;
The boom of dawn that left her sleeping, showing
    The flowers mirrored in the mahogany table.

O my love, if only I were able
    To protract this hour of quiet after passion,
Not ration happiness but keep this door for ever
    Closed on the world, its own world closed within it.

But dawn's waves trouble with the bubbling minute,
    The names of books come clear upon their shelves,
The reason delves for duty and you will wake
    With a start and go on living on your own.

The first train passes and the windows groan,
    Voices will hector and your voice become
A drum in tune with theirs, which all last night
    Like sap that fingered through a hungry tree
Asserted our one night's identity.

The Net

This poem is from Europa and the Bull and Other Poems *by W. R. Rogers, which appeared in 1952. Rogers was at one time a Presbyterian minister in Loughgall, Co. Armagh.*

Quick, woman, in your net
Catch the silver I fling!
O I am deep in your debt,
Draw tight, skin-tight, the string,
And rake the silver in.
No fisher ever yet
Drew such a cunning ring.

Ah, shifty as the fin
Of any fish this flesh
That, shaken to the shin,
Now shoals into your mesh,
Bursting to be held in;
Purse-proud and pebble-hard,
Its pence like shingle showered.

Open the haul, and shake
The fill of shillings free,
Let all the satchels break
And leap about the knee
In shoals of ecstasy.
Guineas and gills will flake
At each gull-plunge of me.

Though all the Angels, and
Saint Michael at their head,
Nightly contrive to stand
On guard about your bed,
Yet none dare take a hand,
But each can only spread
His eagle-eye instead.

But I, being man, can kiss
And bed-spread-eagle too;
All flesh shall come to this,
Being less than angel is,
Yet higher far in bliss
As it entwines with you.

Come, make no sound, my sweet;
Turn down the candid lamp
And draw the equal quilt
Over our naked guilt.

Bluebells for Love

This is a simple little poem by Patrick Kavanagh.

There will be bluebells growing under the big trees
And you will be there and I will be there in May;
For some other reason we both will have to delay
The evening in Dunshaughlin—to please
Some imagined relation,
So both of us came to walk through that plantation.

Maighread Medbh

This is the final stanza of a poem Our Streets, *from*
The Making of a Pagan.

These are our streets.
If you are a woman you must break the mould,
smash the flashy screen
that makes us meat for pricks
and not for joy.
If you are a woman you must fight
to choose to work, to dress, to fuck,
to look straight in the eye,
to stroll and not
Walk faster.

The Big Sycamore

The novel from which this extract is taken was written by
'Joseph Brady' (Monsignor Maurice Browne) and
published in 1958. It tells of the life, and love, of
a schoolmaster in a small village.

It seemed that Maurice was destined for the single life. But an event took place that put an end to such an idea. There is a tradition that he lingered on for thanksgiving after first mass in Letterlee one Sunday in May. Spring was in the air. He looked up from his well-thumbed prayer book. A ray of sunlight flashed through the stain-glass window on the Epistle side, filtered through the crook of St. Patrick's crozier, illumined raven tresses, pin-pointed for one moment a lovely Grecian nose and was reflected back from the irises of two hazel brown eyes set in the kindliest, sweetest face on this earth. The owner of those eyes was walking demurely down the centre aisle. She wore a black cape that emphasised the pallor of her face. Her cheek bones were high, her ears delicately formed. Maurice's heart missed a beat. He closed his prayer book, made a quick genuflection, and was just in time to hold open the swing door that led to the porch. She smiled in salutation, with a twinkle of subtle humour in her eyes. From that smile was shot the Cupid's arrow that pierced the heart of Maurice Fitzgerald. He saw her walk daintily to a pony and trap that waited at the chapel gate. She lifted the flounce of her dress and sprang airily to the cushioned seat. A flick of the whip from the driver and the little pony was away like a flash. A discreet enquiry from a man who was sitting on the chapel wall brought the information that the driver was Jim Whelan of Ballyduggan, a little hamlet that was half way between Mullenaglock and Mullinahone.

Maurice didn't linger long over Maryanne's special Sunday dinner. He went off on what seemed an innocent afternoon stroll towards Mullinahone. As he passed the Finger Post he lilted a plaintive air—John Walshe's 'By the Shannon's dancing water'—to lighten the way. He arrived at Ballyduggan but dared not call to the house of his dreams. An angel in the form of a lively girl of about twelve years was whipping a spinning top as she came along the road from Mullinahone. She was about to enter the gateway of the passage that led to a farmhouse set about one hundred yards from the road. Maurice asked the girl her name.

'Johanna Sullivan,' she replied with a smile.

'What school do you attend?'

'Letterlee.'

'Do you know me?'

'Of course; aren't you Mr. Fitzgerald, the teacher?'

'Will you call to Devoy's tomorrow after school. I stay there,' said Maurice, a little bit confused.

'I will tell Aunt Kate that you want me to call.'

'Who is Aunt Kate?'

'Oh, don't you know. She is home from Loreto Convent. She came home to mind her mother who died two months ago.'

'Is she returning to the convent?'

'Maybe yes, maybe no,' said Johanna, looking very wise. Maurice's face must have registered dismay, because in the very next breath Johanna added, 'I hope not. They would be lost here without her. Three brothers and no one but me to look after them, if their sister goes away.' After a brief pause she said, 'I think she has given up the notion of becoming a nun.'

Hope was re-born. Maurice said, 'Be sure to call after school.' With those words he opened the gate for the little girl, smiled in farewell and set his face for Letterlee.

When Jo entered the Whelan home she said in a breathless voice, 'I met Mr. Fitzgerald, the teacher. He was at the gate. I would have liked to ask him in. He seemed upset.'

'What is he like?' asked Kate.

'Oh, a fine big man with a brown beard. He has only one hand,' was Jo's terse answer.

In a flash Kate remembered the incident of the brown-bearded man holding open the church door that morning. She dismissed the idea that the same man walked all the way from Letterlee just to see the gate-way that led to her house.

In true conspiratorial fashion, Jo said nothing to Kate about Maurice's request to call to his lodgings in Letterlee. Next day after close of school Jo called to Devoy's as arranged. Maurice asked her to come into the room at the rere of the public house. Shanafaddy was resting on the sofa. Maurice hinted that he wanted a quiet talk with Jo Sullivan.

Jo was very mystified. When Tom Devoy left the room, Maurice produced two packets from a locked drawer. One was a bag of 'bull's eyes,' the other was a bulky envelope. Maurice instructed Jo that he didn't want anyone to know that this envelope was for Miss Kate Whelan. Jo at once sampled one of the 'bull's eyes' and went homewards with winged feet—a Mercury with her missive.

With an air of solemnity she beckoned Aunt Kate into the bedroom where both slept. She took from her bosom the large plain envelope and would have waited in the hope of getting a clue to the mystery. But Kate told her to go up to the garden where Jim was sowing the wheat.

'Tell him to call over to Louis Neill when he has finished the sowing. Louis wants him to look at a cow that has gone off her feed since yesterday.'

Jo realised that the time was not opportune for revelations. She went skipping up to the tillage garden.

When Kate was sure that Jo was on her way and not likely to make a last-minute run back to the bedroom for a strong pair of boots or for an old jacket, she slit open the envelope.

She read her first love letter:

Dear Miss Whelan,

Since I saw you walk down the aisle of Letterlee church yesterday, I shall never again know peace of mind until you allow me to speak to you. I want to tell you that, even if you never speak to me, I love you and shall love you to the end of time. A teacher far from home is 'an outcast from kith and kin.' Long has been my weary wandering without one living soul to keep me company. My heart is lonely, and of late I am becoming depressed for lack of true companionship. Although I find the school-children intelligent and dutiful, and the people kind-hearted here at the foot of Slievenamon, yet I feel that I have not been accepted as one of themselves. Sometimes I have been on the point of seeking an appointment elsewhere, but I have been held fast by I know not what invisible prayer. I have even prayed like Saint Paul when he was struck blind on the road to Damascus, 'Lord, what wilt thou have me to do?' Yesterday it seems to me the Good Lord has sent me a sign. I looked up from bended knee towards the altar, and my first impression was of a heavenly being walking down the church. You have the sweetest, kindest, most compassionate face that I have ever seen. I thought —but it was merely my imagination—that you seemed to have emerged from a crucible of suffering, but emerged triumphant. An angel was sent to conduct Tobias to Sarah. Such an angel I met last evening at your gate at Ballyduggan. This angel was whipping a top while she tripped on light fantastic toe, as if at a moment's notice she could have taken flight to the stars. She has promised to be angel or messenger for me. Tobias had to undergo many trials before he received Sarah in marriage. I am prepared to undertake even the impossible and wait a life-time to prove my love for you. This may seem extravagant language, but I am an extravagant person in all except pecuniary matters. For there I have to trim my sails to the wind. A teacher gets little remuneration for hard work. At that I do not grumble. When I lost my right hand at an early age—you must have noticed my affliction—God did not abandon me. In His quiver He protected me and led me on to the teaching profession, which I now believe was my vocation, even if an accident had never befallen me.

It may embarrass you to arrange a meeting with me. I live in a rather squalid public house in which I have no privacy. I leave it to you and our little friend Johanna, or Jo when I am in a hurry, as she quaintly said. Any meeting-place on this earth that you suggest will suit me. May I dare sign myself,

Your devoted admirer,

Maurice Fitzgerald.

Goodbye to the Hill

This extract is from an early work by Lee Dunne, published in 1965; it is a delicately portrayed vision of tentative attraction.

'Well, are you comin' or not?'

She shook her head at him. 'I can't, I have a date with Paddy.'

I didn't look at her in case the surprise showed in my face, but I looked at him and I didn't mind that he hadn't taken my hand. Who needed him, anyway?

'My bike's around Leinster Road,' I said to Maureen.

She put her small hand into the crook of my arm and I looked at your man again. I'll say this for him, he didn't seem all that bothered and I knew that if it had been me I'd have been looking for a hole to crawl into.

'Good night, Willie.'

He grinned the way Douglas Fairbanks did just before he dived into the moat in *The Prisoner of Zenda*, and then he jumped up on the bike right there on the footpath. 'I'll see you around,' he said, and he shot off like a bullet and in a few seconds all we could see was the red hum of his rear reflector as he hit the top of Rathmines Road.

'He's an awful boaster,' Maureen said as we turned the corner into Leinster Road.

She didn't know then and I never told her how much she had helped me that night. To have backed me up when that bastard had tried to shoot me right up the arse was the biggest favour she could have done me. I was sick with the inferiority thing, one of the scars that you were sure to carry if you were born and lived on The Hill. I knew it even then and I hated myself for wallowing in self-pity, but I couldn't do a thing about it. Why me? I used to ask myself. Why couldn't I have been born in a decent house with a father who had a steady job, and so on. And when people rejected me I blamed it on the fact that they knew I was from The Hill. It never occurred to me that they mightn't have liked me anyway. I was sick with it, like I said, and I knew it and whether I could or not, at that time, I didn't try to do anything about it.

I wanted to tell her, there and then, how much I loved her and I think I could have done. The silent painful bit was over, I knew that from the way I felt, but I was afraid I'd frighten her off. So I kept quiet and we walked up the road and she held on to my arm. After a minute I took a deep breath and I moved my arm so that her hand fell free.

'What's the matter, Paddy?'

'I want to hold your hand.'

She put her small white hand in mine and the touch of it was an electric shock and I loved her and I wanted to die on the spot.

'You're a nice fella, aren't you?' She smiled up at me.

'It isn't difficult to be nice to you.'

Well, we were talking, anyway, even if it was a bit strained. The street was dark except where the street lights were, and when we turned into the lane that led up to Mount Drummond it was like the inside of an ink bottle. And still I wouldn't have been surprised if birds had started to chirp along the way.

We stopped without a word being said by a deep garage door-way and I put the bike against the wall. Maureen stood looking up at me and I put the bike against the wall. Like a magnet, she came against me and I kissed her with every bit of feeling and energy that was in me. Her hands went around the back of my neck and she held on to me and her breasts against me were hot pains in my miserable chest.

When she pulled away she looked at me and despite the darkness I could see that she couldn't believe what was happening and it was then that I knew she felt the way I did.

'I'm crazy about you, Maureen. Will you come out with me?'

She nodded without a word, and then pressing against me she tucked her head into my shoulder and I thought that I knew what it was to be really happy for the first time in my life.

Like Any Other Man

This novel by Patrick Boyle, published in 1966, could best be described as rollicking. The extract given illustrates an ambivalent attitude to sexual morality frequently encountered in Ireland.

'Aw, have a heart, Delia. You'd think I never saw you before with your clothes off.'

She opened the door.

'Out!' she said. 'Out! You take too much for granted.' Pushing him out, she slammed the door. He heard the bolt click shut.

For a moment he listened outside but nothing could be heard above the sound of gushing tap water. Moodily he crossed to the bedroom. Got out the whiskey. Poured himself a glass. He was stretched on the bed, sipping his drink, when he heard her call. At once he put down the glass. Rushed to the bathroom door.

'What is it?' he asked.

'The bolt's off,' she said. 'What kept you?'

When he opened the door he could see nothing for the thick cloud of steam. Against this white mist, the green scum of unabsorbed blood obscuring the vision of his eye showed up with startling clarity, shifting and swirling as he looked around. A cud of bitterness rose to his throat. What was he doing here anyway? Acting the penny-boy for a chit of a girl no more than half his age. Running to her if she cracked her fingers. Wasn't there a score of girls in the area, better built and better mannered, to be had for the picking? Girls that would be damned glad to have a leg thrown over them. That wouldn't be treating it as a class of a compliment if they let you mount them. That would be cute and close-mouthed and not disgrace you with a public display of intimacy. God knows, half the countryside could have seen the shameless, brazen antics of her on the cliff tops or deserted beaches or even, so help me, the grass verge of the bloody highway. What was he thinking of, anyway, bringing her to the Bank House? Fouling his own nest. Let this get out and he might as well pack up and go. If she doesn't drive the eyes out of your head with her unbridled craving for cock. Surely to Christ you should know by now that this randy scuttling after a rutting bitch will only bring on another haemorrhage? Have you forgotten, you sore idiot?

From the cloud of steam, her voice nagged:

'Are you deaf? Why are you standing there like a mutton dummy? Can't you answer a civil question?'

'What do you want to know?'

'What kept you? I've asked you a dozen times.'

'Sorry.'

'Come here and soap my back.'

His heart clenched in anguish as he stood beside the bath looking down at her. She was sitting up straight, hands clasped around raised knees. Beads of water glistened on her shoulders. Trickled erratically down the smooth back. Her skin glowed, as though life—fierce, urgent, resolute—seethed and bubbled under a thin envelope of flesh. A lock of hair dangled foolishly over one eye. Her thumbs tapped out upon her left knee the rhythm of a dance number. Young, guileless, terribly vulnerable she looked. An intolerable wave of tenderness overwhelmed him. An urge to comfort. To caress.

He touched her shoulder gently.

'Here,' she said. 'The soap.'

Over her shoulder she handed it to him.

Gravely, conscientiously, he lathered and rubbed, rubbed and lathered, while she complained:

'Go easy, will you. You'll take the skin off my back the way you're scouring it.'

Once, to steady her swaying body, he cupped a hand against one of her breasts. She pushed it away immediately.

'Now-now! No monkey business or out you'll go.'

At last she lay back in the bath, eyes closed, muscles slack, savouring the scented warmth. Dry-mouthed, jaw muscles aching, Simpson stared at the brown nipples rising provocatively from the soapy, scummy water.

At length, she roused herself.

'Get the towel. You can dry me.'

Wrapped in the bath towel, she stamped around impatiently whilst he tried, with a show of nonchalance, to towel down the moist and yielding flesh. She shrugged him away.

'I'll do it myself. You'll be all night at it.'

She dried herself briskly, flung the wet towel on a chair and commenced to dress. Desperately Simpson sought ways to detain her.

'There's no need to ... to rush off so early. It's only—' he glanced at his watch. 'It's just gone ten.'

Head emerging from the waist-band of her skirt, she paused, eyeing him with cagey stare.

'We could have a jar before I drive you home,' he said, wincing at the blatancy of the excuse.

She tugged the skirt down. Pulled and patted it into place.

'If you're planning any hanky-panky,' she said, 'you're wasting your time. I'm going home after one drink.'

She finished dressing and followed him across the landing to the bedroom. Watched as he got out the glasses and the whiskey bottle from the wardrobe.

'You had everything nicely planned,' she said. 'Pity it's too late for me to stay.'

At the dressing-table, back turned to her, he filled out the drinks. One a half-tumblerful. The other a normal measure.

'Water?' he asked over his shoulder.

'Yes.'

Into the smaller drink, he poured from the carafe. Poured till the two measures were level.

'That should do the trick,' he said. 'And a little tincture for myself.'

He tilted a driblet of water into the second glass.

'Here we are,' he said cheerfully, crossing his hands as he picked up the drinks. As he swung round, his hands uncrossed and he passed her the larger drink. Grasping his own glass so that the contents could not be seen, he raised it.

'Bottoms up,' he said, clinking glasses with her.

He drank. Three long slugs.

'That's better,' he said, putting down his empty glass.

Delia was coughing and spluttering.

'Did it go down the wrong way?' he commiserated.

Tears in her eyes, she wheezed:

'Where did you get … that whiskey? … It's fierce strong.'

'Up the town some place. Why? Nothing wrong with it, I hope. Tasted all right to me.'

He filled himself another modest measure. Topped it up with water. Sipped.

'Nothing the matter with that whiskey, as far as I can see. Maybe I put too much water in yours. It's a mistake to drown it, you know.'

She took a cautious sip. Grimaced.

'Awful. Tastes of linoleum.'

'Probably too young. Not manured … I mean matured properly.'

'It seems to be hitting you fast enough. You're stuttering already.'

'I am not.' He drank. A quick gulp. Smacked his lips appreciatively. 'I'll swear it's not a day younger than ten year old. Drink it up and stop acting like a schoolgirl.'

She drank standing, puffing loudly after each swallow.

'You get to like it, don't you?' he said.

'Lino. New lino. Just unrolled. Smelling of cat.' With a final puff of relief, she put down her empty glass. 'Come on now. We're for off.'

'What's your hurry? It's early yet. Plenty of time for another gargle.' He held up the bottle invitingly.

'I don't know. It's dreadful stuff.'

'Tell you what. I'll bring up some milk. That'll kill the taste.'

When he came back, she was sitting on the bed.

'You're very comfortable here,' she said.

He collected the glasses and commenced to mix the drinks as before. One large. One small. A compensating quantity of milk in each. As he crossed his hands he had to look closely to detect which held the most liquor.

'Now,' he said, as he reached her the glass. 'See if that tastes any better.'

She sipped.

'Ummm. Much better.'

She kicked off her shoes. Plumped up the pillow. Stretched her feet out on the quilt.

'Much better.'

She sipped the whiskey and milk, whilst Simpson strove to make small talk. As was his wont, he ran through the alphabet, seeking a topic. *A* is for *amorous*. Too revealing. *B* is for *bunk*. Ditto. *C* is for *cheesecake*. Jesus, I can't get away from it. *D* is for *drunk*. We bloody well hope. He burst out laughing.

'What's so funny?' she asked.

'I was thinking of Vereker.'

'Nothing funny about that little squirt.'

'Ach, it was just something he said. About muzzling a dog.'

Come to think of it, it was a damned good suggestion. There must be one left in that package in the dressing-table drawer. It'll do away with this withdrawal racket. She'll never know the difference. Queer how she thinks that a worse sin than the job itself.

'D'you know. I'll take 'nother drink. Just a teeny weeny one.'

She demonstrated with all-but-joined thumb and forefinger.

She's showing signs of wear and tear, he decided, as he filled her out another huge bumper of whiskey, colouring it with a little splash of milk. This one should work the oracle.

Without shuffling the glasses, he handed her the jaundiced-looking mixture.

'Down the hatch,' he said, throwing back his own watered whiskey.

He stood for a moment, watching her lower the drink in small but steady gulps. Satisfied, he turned away to the dressing-table and commenced to hunt through the drawers. Just as he came across the package, she called:

'Jim, it's getting very hot.'

He pocketed the package. Crossed to the bed.

'Why don't you peel off some of your clothes? You'll feel cooler then.'

Obediently, she commenced to pull off her jumper. With flailing arms she struggled to get it over her head. At last, in a muffled shout, she begged:

'Help me off with this thing, will you?'

He eased it off. She lay back on the pillow, hair tossed, cheeks blotched, eyes glazed.

'Take me home, Jim. Please.'

He bent down and flicked his finger gently across her sweat-soaked forehead.

'Give,' he whispered. 'Don't be nasty.'

'All right. A quickie.'

Blood thundering in his ears, he tore off his clothes. Got out a french letter. Adjusted it with frantic, fumbling fingers.

'I don't feel so good. What's keeping you?' Leaning on one elbow, she peered. Blinking.

'What have you got there? Come here.'

He shuffled nearer.

'Is that what it is? One of those filthy, wicked things?'

She reached out. Ripped it off. Flung it across the room.

'Are you trying to make a hoor of me?' she cried.

Rolling over, she buried her face in the pillow. Sobbing.

'Ooooooooh,' she wailed. 'What am I to do?'

The Faithless Wife

This extract is from a short story by Seán Ó Faoláin in Foreign Affairs and Other Stories, *published in 1976.*

He had now been stalking his beautiful Mlle Morphy, whose real name was Mrs Meehawl O'Sullivan, for some six weeks, and she had appeared to be so amused at every stage of the hunt, so responsive, *entrainante*, even *aguichante*, that he could already foresee the kill over the next horizon. At their first encounter, during the Saint Patrick's Day cocktail party at the Dutch embassy, accompanied by a husband who had not a word to throw to a cat about anything except the scissors and shears that he manufactured somewhere in the West of Ireland, and who was obviously quite ill at ease and drank too much Irish whiskey, what had attracted him to her was not only her splendid Boucher figure (whence his sudden nickname for her, La Morphée), or her copper-coloured hair, her lime-green Irish eyes and her seemingly poreless skin, but her calm, total and subdued elegance: the Balenciaga costume, the peacock-skin gloves, the gleaming crocodile handbag, a glimpse of tiny, lace-edged lawn handkerchief and her dry, delicate scent. He has a grateful eye and nose for such things. It was, after all, part of his job. Their second meeting, two weeks later, at his own embassy, had opened the doors. She came alone.

Now, at last, inside a week, perhaps less, there would be an end to all the probationary encounters that followed—mostly her inventions, at his persistent appeals—those wide-eyed fancy-meeting-you-heres at the zoo, at race-meetings, afternoon cinemas, in art galleries, at more diplomatic parties (once he had said gaily to her, 'The whole diplomacy of Europe seems to circle around our interest in one anoth-er'), those long drives over the Dublin mountains in his Renault coupé, those titillating rural lunches, nose to nose, toe to toe (rural because she quickly educated him to see Dublin as a stock exchange for gossip, a casino of scandal), an end, which was rather a pity, to those charming unforeseen-foreseen, that is to say proposed but in the end just snatched, afternoon *promenades champêtres* under the budding leaves and closing skies of the Phoenix Park, with the first lights of the city springing up below them to mark the end of another boring day for him in Ailesbury Road, Dublin's street of embassies, for her another possibly cosier but, he selfishly hoped, not much more exciting day in her swank boutique on Saint Stephen's Green. Little by little those intimate encounters, those murmured confessions had lifted acquaintance to friendship, to self-mocking smiles over some tiny incident during their last meeting, to eager anticipation of the next, an aimless tenderness twanging to appetite like an arrow. Or, at least, that was how he felt about it all. Any day now, even any hour, the slow countdown, slower than the slow movement of Mendelssohn's Concerto in E Minor, or the most swoony sequence from the Siegfried Idyll, or that floating spun-sugar balloon of Mahler's 'Song of the Earth,' to the music of which on his gramophone he would imagine her smiling sidelong at him as she softly disrobed, and his ingenious playing with her, his teasing and warming of her moment by moment for the roaring, blazing takeoff. To the moon!

Only one apprehension remained with him, not a real misgiving, something nearer to a recurring anxiety. It was that at the last moments when her mind and her body ought to take leave of one another she might take to her heels. It was a fear that flooded him whenever, with smiles too diffident to reassure him, she would once again mention that she was a Roman Catholic, or a Cat, a Papist or a Pape, a convent girl, and once she laughed that during her schooldays in the convent she had actually been made an *Enfant de Marie*. The words never ceased to startle him, dragging him back miserably to his first sexual frustration with his very pretty but unexpectedly proper cousin Berthe Ohnet during his lycée years in Nancy; a similar icy snub a few years later in Quebec; repeated still later by that smack on the face in Rio that almost became a public scandal; memories so painful that whenever an attractive woman nowadays mentioned religion, even in so simple a context as, 'Thank God I didn't buy that hat, or frock, or stock, or mare,' a red flag at once began to flutter in his belly.

169

Obsessed, every time she uttered one of those ominous words he rushed for the reassurance of what he called The Sherbet Test, which meant observing the effect on her of some tentatively sexy joke, like the remark of the young princess on tasting her first sherbet:—'Oh, how absolutely delicious! But what a pity it isn't a sin!' To his relief she not only always laughed merrily at his stories but always capped them, indeed at times so startling him by her coarseness that it only occurred to him quite late in their day that this might be her way of showing her distaste for his diaphanous indelicacies. He had once or twice observed that priests, peasants and children will roar with laughter at some scavenger joke, and growl at even a veiled reference to a thigh. Was she a child of nature? Still, again and again back would come those disturbing words. He could have understood them from a prude, but what on earth did *she* mean by them? Were they so many herbs to season her desire with pleasure in her naughtiness? Flicks of nasty puritan sensuality to whip her body over some last ditch of indecision? It was only when the final crisis came that he wondered if this might not all along have been her way of warning him that she was neither a light nor a lecherous woman, neither a flirt nor a flibber-tigibbet, that in matters of the heart she was *une femme très sérieuse*.

He might have guessed at something like it much earlier. He knew almost from the first day that she was *bien élevée*, her father a judge of the Supreme Court, her uncle a monsignor at the Vatican, a worldly, sport-loving, learned, contriving priest who had persuaded her papa to send her for a finishing year to Rome with the Sisters of the Sacred Heart at the top of the Spanish Steps; chiefly, it later transpired, because the convent was near the *centre hippique* in the Borghese Gardens and it was his right reverend's opinion that no Irish girl could possibly be said to have completed her education until she had learned enough about horses to ride to hounds. She had told him a lot, and most amusingly, about this uncle. She had duly returned from Rome to Dublin, and whenever he came over for the hunting, he always rode beside her. This attention had mightily flattered her until she discovered that she was being used as a cover for his uncontrollable passion for Lady Kinvara and Loughrea, then the master, some said the mistress, of the Clare-Galway hounds.

'How old were you then?' Ferdy asked, fascinated.

'I was at the university. Four blissful, idling years. But I got my degree. I was quick. And,' she smiled, 'good-looking. It helps, even with professors.'

• •

Their lovemaking was not as he had foredreamed it. She hurled her clothes to the four corners of the room, crying out, 'And about time too! Ferdy, what the hell have you been fooling around for during the last six weeks?' Within five minutes she smashed him into bits. In her passion she was more like a lion than a lioness. There was nothing about her either titillating or erotic, indolent or indulgent, as wild, as animal, as unrestrained, as simple as a forest fire. When, panting beside her, he recovered enough breath to speak he expressed his surprise that one so cool, so ladylike in public could be so different in private. She grunted peacefully and said in her muted brogue, 'Ah, shure, dürling, everything changes in the beddaroom.'

He woke at three twenty-five in the morning with that clear bang so familiar to everybody who drinks too much after the chimes of midnight, rose to drink a pint of cold water, lightly opened his curtains to survey the pre-dawn May sky and, turning towards the bed, saw the pallid streetlamp's light fall across her sleeping face, as calm, as soothed, as innocently sated as a baby filled with its mother's milk. He sat on the side of the bed looking down at her for a long time, overcome by the terrifying knowledge that, for the first time in his life, he had fallen in love.

The eastern clouds were growing as pink as petals while they drank the coffee he had quietly prepared. Over it he arranged in unnecessarily gasping whispers for their next meeting the following afternoon—'*This* afternoon!' he said joyously—at three twenty-five, henceforth his Mystic Hour for Love, but only on the strict proviso that he would not count on her unless she had set three red geraniums in a row on the windowsill of her boutique before three o'clock and that she, for her part, must divine a tragedy if the curtains of his flat were not looped high when she approached at three twenty o'clock. He could, she knew, have more easily checked with her by telephone, but also knowing how romantically, voluptuously, erotically minded he was she accepted with an indulgent amusement what he obviously considered ingenious devices for increasing the voltage of passion by the trappings of conspiracy. To herself she thought, 'Poor boy! He's been reading too many dirty books.'

Poem for Marie

This is a totally charming poem by Séamus Heaney
for his wife, Marie. It is taken from Death of a Naturalist,
published in 1966.

Love, I shall perfect for you the child
Who diligently potters in my brain
Digging with heavy spade till sods were piled
Or puddling through muck in a deep drain.

Yearly I would sow my yard-long garden.
I'd strip a layer of sods to build the wall
That was to exclude sow and pecking hen.
Yearly, admitting these, the sods would fall.

Or in the sucking clabber I would splash
Delightedly and dam the flowing drain
But always my bastions of clay and mush
Would burst before the rising autumn rain.

Love, you shall perfect for me this child
Whose small imperfect limits would keep breaking:
Within new limits now, arrange the world
Within our walls, within our golden ring.

Act of Union

This is a rather different type of love poem by Heaney, still, however, delicate.

I

To-night, a first movement, a pulse,
As if the rain in bogland gathered head
To slip and flood: a bog-burst,
A gash breaking open the ferny bed.
Your back is a firm line of eastern coast
And arms and legs are thrown
Beyond your gradual hills. I caress
The heaving province where our past has grown.
I am the tall kingdom over your shoulder
That you would neither cajole nor ignore.
Conquest is a lie. I grow older
Conceding your half-independent shore
Within whose borders now my legacy
Culminates inexorably.

II

And I am still imperially
Male, leaving you with the pain,
The rending process in the colony,
The battering ram, the boom burst from within.
The act sprouted an obstinate fifth column
Whose stance is growing unilateral.
His heart beneath your heart is a wardrum
Mustering force. His parasitical
And ignorant little fists already
Beat at your borders and I know they're cocked
At me across the water. No treaty
I foresee will salve completely your tracked
And stretchmarked body, the big pain
That leaves you raw, like opened ground, again.

Valediction

It is difficult to decide whether to laugh at the light-heartedness of the two simple first lines of this poem by Séamus Heaney or to sympathise with his self-confessed incompleteness.

Lady with the frilled blouse
And simple tartan skirt,
Since you have left the house
Its emptiness has hurt
All thought. In your presence
Time rode easy, anchored
On a smile; but absence
Rocked love's balance, unmoored
The days. They buck and bound
Across the calendar
Pitched from the quiet sound
Of your flower-tender
Voice. Need breaks on my strand;
You've gone, I am at sea.
Until you resume command
Self is in mutiny.

On Not Being Your Lover

This poem is by Medbh McGuckian.

Your eyes were ever brown, the colour
Of time's submissiveness. Love nerves
Or a heart, beat in their world of
Privilege, I had not yet kissed you
On the mouth.

But I would not say, in my un-freedom
I had weakly drifted there, like the
Bone-deep blue that visits and decants
The eyes of our children:

How warm and well-spaced their dreams
You can tell from the sleep-late mornings
Taken out of my face! Each lighted
Window shows me cardiganed, more desolate
Than the garden, and more hallowed
Than the hinge of the brass-studded
Door that we close, and no one opens,
That we open and no one closes.

Love Poem

This 'Love Poem' is from Michael Longley's An Exploded View *of the period 1968–72.*

I

You define with your perfume
Infinitely shifting zones
And print in falls of talcum
The shadow of your foot.

II

Gossamers spin from your teeth,
So many light constructions
Describing as with wet wings
The gully under my tongue.

III

These wide migrations begin
In our seamier districts—
A slumdweller's pigeons
Released from creaking baskets.

Love Poem

This 'Love Poem', on the other hand, is from Michael Longley's
Man Lying on a Wall *of 1972–75.*

If my nose could smell only
You and what you are about,
If my fingertips, tongue, mouth
Could trace your magnetic lines,
Your longitudes, latitudes,
If my eyes could see no more
Than dust accumulating
Under your hair, your skin's
Removals and departures,
The glacial progression
Of your fingernails, toenails,
If my ears could hear nothing
But the noise of your body's
Independent processes,
Lungs, heartbeat, intestines,
Then I would be lulled in sleep
That soothes for a lifetime
The scabby knees of boyhood,
And alters the slow descent
Of the scrotum towards death.

The Pornographer

This short extract is from John McGahern's novel of 1979;
the extract, incidentally, is an example of the work
of the eponymous hero.

'That bastard McKenzie knew I wanted to be away early. He made me go right back over the last two letters. You could feel his breathing as he pushed up to me to point out the errors,' Mavis declares as she flings off her coat.

'It's perfectly ridiculous, darling, and all your own fault. I've always said you should give up that filthy job and come to work for me full time.'

'I know what working full time for you would mean. It'd mean I'd never be off the job.'

'I can't think of anything more delightful,' the Colonel beams. 'We've still almost three hours to the flight time. What would you like to have, darling? A g-and-t?'

'With plenty of ice,' she says kicking her shoes off and stretching full length on the wine-coloured chaise longue. She has on a black wrap-around leather skirt and a white cotton blouse buttoned up the front and fringed with pale ruffles.

He lets his fingers dangle a moment among the ruffles and she smiles and blows him a low kiss but says firmly, 'Make the drinks first.'

When he comes back with the drinks he sits beside her on the chaise longue. 'We'll have time for a little old something before going to the airport.'

'I could do with a good screw myself.'

As he sips at the drink, 'It is my great pleasure,' he slowly undoes the small white buttons of the blouse, and slips the catch at the back so that the ripe breasts fall.

Seeing his trousers bulge, she finishes the gin, reaches over and draws down the zip. She has to loosen the belt though before she can pull 'my old and trusty friend' free. The Colonel shivers as she strokes him lightly along the helmet, lifts it to her mouth. Uncontrollably he loosens the ties of the skirt, pushes the leather aside to feast his eyes on the pale silk and softer, paler skin. With trembling fingers he undoes the small buttons, and the mound of soft hair, his pussy, his Venus mound, breathes free between the rich thighs.

'Why don't we go into the bedroom, I'm tired,' she says.

He picks her up like a feather and carries her into the room, feeling as if he could carry her without hands on the very strength of his bayonet of blue Toledo.

'I want to see that gorgeous soft mound on high,' he says and lifts up her buttocks and draws down a pillow beneath, and feasts on the soft raised mound, the pink of the inside lips under the hair. When she puts her arms round his shoulders the stiff pink nipples are pulled up like thumbs, and he stoops and takes them turn and turn about in his teeth and draws them up till she moans. Slowly he opens the lips in the soft mound on the pillows, smears them in their own juice, and slowly moves the helmet up and down in the shallows of the mound. As he pulls up the nipples in his teeth, moving slowly on the pillow between the thighs now thrown wide, she cries, 'Harder, hurt me, do anything you want with me, I'm crazy for it.'

She moans as she feels him go deeper within her, swollen and sliding on the oil seeping out from the walls. 'O Jesus,' she cries as she feels it searching deeper within her, driving faster and faster.

'Fuck me, O fuck me, O my Jesus,' he feels her nails dig into his back as the hot seed spurts deliciously free, beating into her. And when they are quiet he says, 'You must let me,' and his bald head goes between her thighs on the pillow, his rough tongue parting the lips to lap at the juices, then to tease the clitoris till she starts to go crazy again.

'I have to shower,' she says firmly, as much to herself as to him. 'We haven't all that much time.' 'We'll shower together,' he lifts her and carries her into the bathroom. She wraps her thighs round his hips as the iron-hard rod slips again within her. Once he pulls the switchcord they can be seen in all the walled mirrors, and she watches herself move at the hips, over and back on the rod, feeling it hard and enormous within her. 'We have to hurry,' she says. Then, slowly, pressed back against the steamed mirror, she feels the remorseless throb within her, and gripping him tighter she opens and closes to suck each pulse until she shouts out, 'O Jesus,' as she feels the melting into her own pulsing go deeper and deeper, as gradually the world returns to the delicious scalding water showering down on them.

Exhibitionist

Eavan Boland is one of the most distinguished contemporary female poets. This piece is from In Her Own Image, *published in 1980.*

I wake to dark,
a window slime of dew.
Time to start

working
from the text,
making

from this trash
and gimmickry
of sex

my aesthetic:
a hip first,
a breast,

a slow
shadow strip
out of clothes

that bushelled me
asleep.
What an artist am I!

Barely light
and yet—
cold shouldering

clipped laurel,
nippling the road—
I subvert

sculpture,
the old mode:
I skin

I dimple clay,
I flesh,
I rump stone.

This is my way,
to strip and strip
until

my dusk flush,
nude shade,
hush

of hip,
back bone,
thigh

blacks light
and I
become the night.

What stars
I harvest
to my dark!

Cast down
Lucifers,
spruce

businessmen,
their eyes
cast down.

I have them now.
I'll teach them now.
I'll show them how

in offices,
their minds
blind on files,

the view
blues through
my curves and arcs.

They are
a part
of my dark plan:

Into the gutter
of their lusts
I burn

the shine
of my flesh.
Let them know

for a change
the hate
and discipline,

the lusts
that prison
and the light that is

unyielding
frigid
constellate.

For Roberta in the Garden

This is a little poem by John Hewitt for his wife from
Loose Ends, *published in 1983.*

I know when you are at your happiest,
kneeling on mould, a trowel in your glove;
you raise your eyes and for a moment rest;
you turn a young-girl's face, like one in love.

Intent, entranced, this hour, in gardening,
surely to life's bright process you belong.
I wonder, when you pause, you do not sing,
for such a moment surely has its song.

Flesh ... the Greatest Sin

*This portion of the poem 'Flesh ... the Greatest Sin' by Eithne
Strong, published in 1980, makes a fine sociological comment
on the way romance, love and sex were all too
commonly regarded in Ireland.*

From the first, Voices of Authority had forbidden:
Deny flesh: Mortify. Abnegate. Voices had wrought
fear: Remember Hell. Remember Mary, the Immaculate,
conceived *without sin*. Remember. Ellen
remembered that flesh was sin, flesh laid on flesh brought
stirrings that meant Hell. The old voices sounded always
unrelentingly in her life. Do not indulge. Punish.
Crucify self. And the new: from the pulpit, now,
the priest frenzied out his loathing; vituperation
of flesh convulsed him near seizure.

At night
he searched bushes
long grass, ditches,
torch and stick flesh—flash.
He howled he would exterminate impurity;
his duty to insist how putrid the body,
how easily the devil's. He, God's anointed,
ordained to work for the purest Virgin,
would not, he screamed, could not
rest, where sinful horrors stank.
He battered all the courting nooks;
no couples met unknown.

Long since terrorised to non-response, flesh
of Ellen could not accommodate to this unwelcome licence
called Conjugal Right: it established her bewilderment,
recoil, hate, but never joy; an insidious
antagonist, it swelled her with pregnant ills,
weighed thick her ankles, but it was
ecclesiastically endorsed, Church backed,
and Ellen lived Church-awed.
Confusion gave her a lashing tongue so that
scorn became her general reflex
to every sign of the allowed act,
Yet the enemy took access; it was the law.

And she conceived with no rejoicing. Five times.
The two who lived she reared with all respect
to received authority; they must be primed
against the coils of flesh, made know the body should
be fed only for work to be done, not for gratification;
her scorn spat the vileness of men, the grossness, lust:
'... and haven't we heard what to do about scandal? pluck
out the eye, cut off the hand—clear enough, isn't it?
Where there is the bad drop, a man starts with that taint;
he ought to keep an iron clamp on the blood;
people with the bad drop take a filthy satisfaction,
using their wives with Conjugal Right.'

She spewed her contempt on self-indulgent ancestors,
grandfathers, uncles, cousins. Whenever possible
she talked with women, low secret colloquies
to do with tumours, wombs, female parts not to be named
before men: exclusive privacies uttering miscarriages,
haemorrhages, unending press of pregnancies,
loaded with moan, with women's rage at their abuse.
In living dread, however, of a vengeful Maker,
they always deluged speech with God-be-praised,
named His saints, called on His mother,
wishfully protected, by this summoned phalanx
of sanctity, from eternally punishable blasphemy.

All was God's will; how, then, place demanding men?
They were a different thing. Dilemma. Ellen
arranged, for her satisfaction, a public placebo:
relishing her cronies' rage, she, contrarily,
did not, abroad, indict her man; what she
held legitimate pride required it must be thought
she had the best; to impress, therefore, amid
the women, the scope of her domain, she fabricated
many a subterfuge, mostly doing so well that
she believed her own deceit. Pride—this kind,
she did not rate as one of the Seven Deadly—
was to her imperative, a sort of personal oxygen.

She gave, then, to be known
that Thomas, her Tom, was
exemplary, 'good', meaning
'never looking for any of *that*'
the baneful cause of other women's woes.
Her various pains and aches
she would attribute publicly
to reasons different from theirs,
keeping for domiciled fury
the verbal annihilation
that always met
any rearing signs in Tom.

As for him,
his parts lifted no more;
banished
from speech, sight, touch,
to an eliminatory limbo,
never again to know
the light of free acknowledgement.
Whenever
bombardments shattered,
or even threatened,
Thomas always
took to the moor.

The Railway Station Man

This is a slightly uncharacteristic extract from Jennifer Johnston's novel The Railway Station Man, *published in 1984.*

He closed the car door quietly and pointed down the hill. Jack nodded and drove off.

They lay on the sofa in front of the fire, half drunk with love and wine. The flickering light from the fire made their bodies seem to writhe, but they were in fact quite still, quite peaceful. They heard nothing but the sound of their own breathing, the pumping of two hearts. They heard no car, no latch click, no steps in the hall. The first moment they were aware of Jack's presence was when he opened the sitting-room door and switched on the light.

'Mother ... oh Jesus God!'

Helen stared, confused across the back of the sofa for what seemed like a long time before she gathered into her mind what was happening.

'Jack.'

She stood up, fastening the buttons down the front of her shirt.

'You never told me you were coming down.'

She bent and picked her skirt from the floor and stepped into it.

Roger sat up, rubbing at his eye as if it were paining him.

'Hello, Jack.' His voice was composed.

Helen picked up his trousers and dropped them on top of him.

'You should have let me know you were coming. I think we've probably eaten all the food.'

'I don't need food. I tried to phone but I couldn't get through,' he lied.

She nodded, not believing him.

'I think I'll just ...' He backed out of the room into the hall ... 'just, bathroom.'

He disappeared and they heard him running up the stairs. Roger got up from the sofa and pulled his trousers on.

'I suppose we've shocked him,' said Helen. 'Oh dear ... I hope we haven't appalled him.' She giggled. 'His face was appalled. I hope he doesn't do anything awful up there.'

'Don't be silly, Helen, he'll just recover his equilibrium and then he'll come down. You'd better give him a large drink.'

Helen was punching at the cushions on the sofa.

'Is this sordid?' she asked, suddenly anxious, 'or really a bit funny? It's not very dignified.'

'It would have been one hell of a lot less dignified if he'd arrived ten minutes earlier. A whisky? I'm having a whisky. To induce the correct light-hearted approach.'

'I'll stick to wine.'

Jack came into the room.

'Whisky?' asked Roger. Jack nodded abruptly and walked over to Helen who was standing with her back to the fire.

'What's all this anyway?'

'What's all what?'

'This ... this ...' he pointed towards the sofa.

'Have your drink, Jack dear. There's no need for you to get all worked up.'

'I'm not worked up.'

Roger came across the room and put a glass of whisky into his hand.

'I'm embarrassed. I'm ashamed. For God's sake, I might have had someone with me.'

'But you didn't,' said Helen. 'And anyway if you'd said you were coming down we would have behaved in a more appropriate way.'

'Would you mind very much opening this bottle of wine for your mother? I can't use this corkscrew.'

'Yes, I do mind. My mother's had enough to drink all ready. I can see that by looking at her.'

'You're being a bit grotesque,' said Helen, coldly.

'Grotesque. I'm being grotesque. That's good. Do you know how grotesque you're being? Nauseatingly grotesque.'

'Jack ...' She put out a hand and touched his shoulder. He shuddered her hand away.

'Don't you touch me.'

Roger took Helen's hand in his.

'You'll have to get over your nausea, young man, because your mother and I love each other and ...'

'Love ... what do you mean love?'

'I'm sorry that you don't know the meaning of the word yourself.'

'She didn't love my father. How can she love someone like you? You're both making fools of yourselves.'

Helen uncoupled her hand from Roger's.

'You go home, darling. Jack will pull himself together and then we'll talk about all this. Just Jack and I will talk about it.' She smiled at him and nodded her head.

'Are you sure?'

'Quite sure.'

She put her arms around his neck and kissed his mouth.

'I love you.'

He held her for a moment.

'Yes,' he said.

Night Shift

This extract, both delicate and charming, is from
Dermot Bolger's novel of 1985.

H
e turned the front key gently in the lock and listened for a moment before tiptoeing down the hall, breathing in the smell of floor polish and the stale reminder of cooking, across the shining tiles in the kitchen and out again into the privacy of the back garden. The early light seemed to hover over the garden with a tactile clarity, focused in long rays through the branches of the trees and lighting up the grass like the rich touched-up colours of a film. Donal's shoes slipped on the dew of the wild lawn as he tried to avoid crunching over the freshly-laid gravel path. The caravan stood in the bottom corner of the garden with a thick overgrown hedge spilling out from the back of it and a lilac tree overshadowing the roof on one side. In the hedge a single bird was testing the airwaves. The first lilac buds were starting to blister the pale bark along the slender branches. Just ten months ago he remembered picking a vast bunch for her as she stood below him in her school uniform catching the stems excitedly. Lilac was short-lived, a firework caught in a branch that burned up in slow motion.

He turned the handle of the door and stepped quietly inside. The light straining through the tinted skylight was fern-coloured. It nestled in a green frame around her head on the pillow as she slept with her limbs tucked up into a ball. Her fair hair was tousled over her eyes and her face so relaxed and abandoned in sleep that she could easily pass for sixteen, her age when they had first met in the swirling heat of a dancehall two years before. In the fragile light of early morning it seemed impossible that such a childlike frame could itself have been carrying his child for nearly four months.

Perhaps it was all a dream. There was choking in his throat as he watched her which he knew was love. It burned inside of him, as

189

physical a sensation as exhaustion or hunger, and yet a different, insatiable feeling that gnawed within like a growth he could do nothing to control. She was so china-doll-like as he stood there dirty and tired that he watched over her with a sense, almost, of awe.

If she was awake when he came in Donal scolded her, yet when she slept on like this, without acknowledging his presence, he always felt a sense of disappointment and, unaccountably, a tremor of unease, as if he were an intruder who had stumbled upon an intimate and private scene. Six weeks of marriage had not adjusted him to the tiny insignificant moments of shared life. All around him in the caravan were the possessions they had begun to accumulate on expeditions to the shopping centre together, which Donal dreaded. He knew his presence was not needed, but that Elizabeth wanted him to share in every purchase as if each of them were indirectly a bond bringing them closer together. So he moved among the pots and the tea sets, the sheets and the basins on Saturday afternoons when he would normally have been playing football or enjoying an extended lie-on after the week. But behind his slightly embarrassed impatience on these trips he was proud of the small world they had built up in such a short space of time, the few possessions that were to be the foundations for a life thrust upon them.

He undressed and folded a blanket over the window to dull the light before pulling back the sheets. She was wearing her light white nightdress, rumpled up over her legs. He lay down beside her in the warmth of the sheets, feeling the softness of her skin against his like ointment on a wound. Still she didn't wake, although her hot body stirred, protesting at the intrusion of cold flesh, and she half turned over on to her front, drawing the bedclothes back towards her. He lay clumsily against her back, watching each breath form and break within her rising shoulders. Four months ago the idea of being able to share a bed openly with her without her two married brothers chasing him around Dublin with shotguns would have appeared both wonderful and impossible. As it was, looking back, he had probably been lucky to escape with his life. He was finding that if he desired something strongly enough he normally got it, but never in the way he had imagined or planned. On some mornings the door of the caravan closed behind him like a coffin lid, confining his life to this small space just when he had begun to realise the scope of it. For eight hours, through darkness into dawn, he had sweated so her turned back could fall and rise through dreams. Exhaustion suddenly made him bitter and disappointed. He could manage without anyone. He was completely alone.

The rush of cold air woke him. He reached out, clutching at space, as if a part of his body he had only been dimly aware of had been torn from him without warning. His lips formed her name in the headlong panic of waking. He could see the back of her fair hair as she leaned over the side of the narrow mattress being sick as quietly as possible. His anger was gone, replaced by a jaded and helpless concern. Needing some role to frame his emotions lest he break down, he held her shoulders, squeezing them softly until she leaned her head back against him. She turned and quickly burrowed her body against his and kissed his naked shoulder. He held her tightly in his arms and gazed up at the discoloured clouds through the skylight. Then he ran his fingers along her back, crumpling her nightdress smoothly down, and said, 'Lie back, I'll make you some tea.'

She snuggled more tightly against him and whispered, 'It came over me so suddenly I couldn't even get out of bed. You should have woken me, Donal. You know I always want to be awake when you come in from that place. I missed you; don't move, Donal, just hold me please.'

Out After Dark

This amusing and—as far as attitudes in Ireland are concerned—historically credible extract is from Hugh Leonard's novel of 1989.

When I was twenty-two and a rebellious teenager (we mature late in Ireland), I wrote the first and only chapter of a novel to be called, devastatingly, *Sex on Thursdays*.

It was not as sensational in intent as the title might suggest: quite simply, when the annual mission—the Retreat, we called it—came to our town, the preachers invariably chose Thursdays for the homily on immodest and immoral behaviour, for it was then that domestic servants had their evening off and could attend church. In those well-ordered days when feminism had still to cut its milk teeth, no one questioned the bald assumption that girls up from the country and in service were so much ripe fruit, helpless on the bough and palpitating for damnation.

Everyone enjoyed the Thursday sermon. On that one evening in the year the parishioners could hear sex being talked about without worrying that it might be a sin to listen. Plain speaking was *de rigueur*. The Jesuits, when they came to Dalkey, were too effete for a town that liked its religion to be the spiritual equivalent of a bowl of stirabout or lashings of bacon and spuds. 'Too much old codology,' my mother once daringly said under her breath—and the Franciscans extolled charity and compassion, neither of which virtue had ever commended itself to the Irish ethos. The star performers were the Redemptorists, who promised the impure of heart an eternity on the hottest hob of hell. 'And, as for those who touch their *bodies* ...!' a missionary would hiss, his own eyes like burning coals, and the entire congregation crooned in an ecstasy of terror.

The idea for the book was the imaginary collision of two quite unconnected events. One of these was the birth of twins to a girl whose name, Honor, was in the circumstances inappropriate, given that the father was unknown, unhonoured (except in the punning sense) and conspicuously unsung. She was not, by the way, a domestic servant, and so the title, *Sex on Thursdays*, was a rank imposture. She was an attractive girl, with shapely legs superb in stockings that had come out of a bottle, with only slightly askew pencil-drawn seams—this was in 1949, when clothes were still rationed. Whenever I passed her on Hyde Road as she trundled a rickety pram with a small bald head protruding from either end, I pictured myself pencilling her stockings on for her, and my lower abdomen tied itself in such tumescent knots that I was obliged to hang on for modesty's sake to the Fannings' pebble-dashed wall. What was worse, her seeming unconcern at the world's opinion suggested that she might actually have enjoyed her misfortune and spiced my fantasies with images of such unbridled abandon that I went on clinging to the wall until old Fanning appeared at his front window and made feck-off gestures of great savagery.

Our town is only nine miles from O'Connell Bridge, and so, even in those backward times, we considered ourselves not unworldly. Sex, as we all knew, was the worst sin of all, but a single biological mishap could be borne stoically. Twins, however, were not to be glossed over. Quality is commonly deemed to be more important than quantity, but our then parish priest did not apply this criterion to illegitimate births. Contrary to both good taste and theology, he got it into his head that in Honor's case the sin was doubled.

Mo Mhíle Stór

This poem by Nuala Ní Dhomhnaill is from the collection Pharaoh's Daughter. *The English translation is by Séamus Heaney.*

I dtús mo shaoil do mheallais mé
i dtráth m'óige, trí mo bhoige.
Thuigis go maith
go bhféadfaí mo cheann a chasadh
le trácht ar chúirteanna aoldaite,
ar chodladh go socair i gcuilteanna
de chlúmh lachan,
ar lámhainní de chraiceann éisc.

Ansan d'imís ar bord loinge,
chuireas mo mhíle slán i do choinne.
Chuireas suas le bruíon is le bearradh
ó gach taobh; bhí tráth ann
go bhféadfainn mo chairde a chomhaireamh
ar mhéireanta aon láimhe amháin,
ach ba chuma.
Thugais uait cúrsa an tsaoil
is d'fhillis abhaile.

Tháinig do long i dtír
ar mo leaba.
Chlúdaíos le mil thú
is chonac go raibh do ghruaig
fachta liath is díreach.

Fós i mo chuimhní
tánn tú bachallach,
tá dhá chocán déag i do chúl buí
cas.

. . . .

I was under your spell from the start:
I was young, I was soft,
and you well knew you could turn my head
with your talk about whitewashed courts
and big long sleeps on a duck-down bed
and gloves made out of the skins of fish.

When you sailed away
my goodbyes were the gulls in your wake.
I put up with rows and with blame
from every side; there was a time
when I could number my friends
on the fingers of one hand.

You sailed through life, you came back home,
your boat beached on my bed.
As I covered you all in honey,
I saw your hair had gone grey
and straight;
but in my memory the curls grew on,
twelve coils in the ripening
crop on your head.

Oileán

This poem by Nuala Ní Dhomhnaill is also from the collection
Pharaoh's Daughter; *the translation is by John Montague.*

Oileán is ea do chorp
i lár na mara móire.
Tá do ghéaga spréite ar bhraillín
gléigeal os farraige faoileán.

Toibreacha fíoruisce iad t'uisí
tá íochtar fola orthu is uachtar meala.
Thabharfaidís fuarán dom
i lár mo bheirfin
is deoch slánaithe
sa bhfiabhras.

Tá do dhá shúil
mar locha sléibhe
lá breá Lúnasa
nuair a bhíonn an spéir
ag glinniúint sna huiscí.
Giolcaigh scuabacha iad t'fhabhraí
ag fás faoina gciumhais.

Is dá mbeadh agam báidín
chun teacht faoi do dhéin,
báidín fiondruine,
gan barrchleite amach uirthi
ná bunchleite isteach uirthi
ach aon chleite amháin
droimeann dearg
ag déanamh ceoil
dom fhéin ar bord,

thógfainn suas
na seolta boga bána
bogóideacha; threabhfainn
trí fharraigí arda
is thiocfainn chughat
mar a luíonn tú
uaigneach, iathghlas,
oileánach.

• • • • • • • • • • • • • • • •

Your nude body is an island
asprawl on the ocean bed. How
beautiful your limbs, spread-
eagled under seagulls' wings!

Spring wells, your temples,
deeps of blood, honey crests.
A cooling fountain you furnish
in the furious, sweltering heat
and a healing drink
when feverish.

Your two eyes gleam
like mountain lakes
on a bright Lammas day
when the sky sparkles
in dark waters.
Your eyelashes are reeds
rustling along the fringe.

And if I had a tiny boat
to waft me towards you,
a boat of findrinny,
not a stitch out of place
from top to bottom
but a single plume
of reddish brown
to play me on board,

To hoist the large white
billowing sails; thrust
through foaming seas
and come beside you
where you lie back,
wistful, emerald,
islanded.

I Cannot Lie Here

*This poem is a translation from the Irish of Nuala Ní
Dhomhnaill. Fortunately there exists a selection of the poems of
Nuala Ní Dhomhnaill, translated by Michael Hartnett,
published in 1986.*

I cannot lie here anymore
in your aroma—
with your pillowed mouth
asnore,
your idle hand
across my hip
not really caring
whether I exist.

I'm not upset
because you ignore me
nor because our happy summer
washes over me—
it's not the bedside flowers
that intoxicate
but your body your aroma,
a blend of blood and earth.

I'll get up from the bed
and put on my clothes
and leave with the carkeys
from your fist stolen
and drive to the city.

At nine tomorrow
you'll get a call
telling you where to go
to pick up your car—
but I cannot lie here anymore
where your aroma laps—
because I'll fall in love with you,
(perhaps)

Double Negative

*This droll poem, describing the kind of situation most of us
have experienced at least once, is from Richard Murphy's*
New Selected Poems, *published in 1985.*

You were standing on the quay
Wondering who was the stranger on the mailboat
While I was on the mailboat
Wondering who was the stranger on the quay

Displaced Person

This poem is also by Richard Murphy.

Those years ago, when I made love to you,
    With fears I was afraid you knew,
    To grow strong I'd pretend to be
A boy I'd loved, loving yourself as me.
I played his part so open-eyed that you
    Believed my artful ploy was true.
    To show I'd nothing false to hide
And make you feel the truth of love I lied.
The love of truth made me confess, and died
    Exposing my hermetic guide,
    A youth found loitering in the mart
Of memory's torn-down inner-city heart.
I feel betrayed by dead words that decide
    If head or tail be certified.
    Dear girl, come back and take a new
Lover in me, let him make love to you.

Afterlove

This poem by Moya Cannon is from the collection Oar.

How could I have forgotten
the sickness,
the inescapability.
My strange love,
it frightens my life.
We sail high seas

and watch the voyages of stars.
Sometimes they collide.
Did you know, you make my head flame.
Blue flames and purple flames leap about my head.
I had once a thousand tongues,
but tonight,
my head is crashing through the sky,
my head is flaming on a dish.

My love,
carry it in carefully.
My love,
carry it in with trumpets.

Parable Jones

This is a very short and amusing excerpt from
The Public World of Parable Jones *by Dominic Behan.*

Parable recalled the excitement of the confessional. He remembered as a kid wanking when he felt there wasn't enough sin in his week to earn a proper penance. Didn't want to waste the confessor's time. And then the fascination of the priest's anger. How dare he abuse himself in such a way! But young Parable didn't think of it as self-abuse. He thought he treated himself very well: twice a day and three times on a Friday—because he knew he wouldn't be able to do it again until after mass on Sunday.

And were the Kimmage clergy stone deaf to all the young men going blind in the right hand? Every Friday evening an adolescence of boys would be outscreaming each other in the agony of ecstasy. Behind the wall in Jameson's field and within an ejaculation of the chapel. The place smelled more of fish than did Aberdeen market. All changed now since rationalism had taken all the sin out of masturbation, and the Hierarchy commanded a sublimation of sex. Changed utterly: a terrible beauty was bored.

Felicity in Turin

This poem, both amusing and sensitive, is from Paul Durcan's
Daddy, Daddy, *published in 1990.*

We met in the Valentino in Turin
And travelled down through Italy by train,
Sleeping together.
I do not mean having sex.
I mean sleeping together.
Of which sexuality is,
And is not, a part.
It is this sleeping together
That is sacred to me.
This yawning together.
You can have sex with anyone
But with whom can you sleep?

I hate you
Because having slept with me
You left me.

White Light

This poem by Mary Dorcey is from the collection
Moving into the Spaced Cleared by Our Mothers.

White light   dark inside me
light growing whiter   inside me
growing whiter   inside me   whiter
than white   growing dark inside
though I did not know it
then   and now   why now?

And you were kind to me when?
Kind smiling   tender
my kind   a kiss was a comfort   a prayer
a huddle against darkness   growing
whiter and white light inside.

Was I not kind back
was I not   was I not?
Did I hurt not knowing
did I hurt?
Hurting so much myself.
Hurting we all hurt
all of us together
fighting the darkness
growing whiter.

Love   you called love
love   love   lover
love me   love me   love me.
Is there another?
the old cry
Is there another than this cry?
than this one   always
huddling together
darkness growing   love me
love me   love me.

And you did
love
you did by any standards—
you did in your way
love me—
not in my way
not in my way
lover.

The Third Party

This is a brief excerpt from a story included in William Trevor's Family Sins and Other Stories. *It illustrates how difficult certain romantic situations can become in Ireland.*

'Good luck.' Boland raised his glass. He had softened the colour of the whiskey by adding twice as much water. 'You never drink this early in the day, I suppose?' he said, constrainedly polite. 'Well, very wise. That's very sensible: I always say it.'

'I thought it mightn't be a drinking occasion.'

'I couldn't face you without a drink in, Lairdman.'

'I'm sorry about that.'

'You've lifted my wife off me. That isn't an everyday occurrence, you know.'

'I'm sorry—'

'It would be better if you didn't keep saying that.'

Lairdman, who was in the timber business, acknowledged the rebuke with a sideways wag of his head. The whole thing was awkward, he confessed, he hadn't slept a wink the night before.

'You're a Dubliner, she tells me,' Boland said, the same politeness to the fore. 'You make blockboard: there's money in that, no doubt about it.'

Lairdman was offended. She'd described her husband as clumsy but had added that he wouldn't hurt a fly. Already, five minutes into the difficult encounter, Lairdman wasn't so sure about that.

'I don't like Dublin,' Boland continued. 'I'll be frank about it. I never have. I'm a small-town man, but of course you'll know.'

He imagined his wife feeding her lover with information about his provincialism. She liked to tell people things; she talked a great deal. Boland had inherited a bakery in the town he had referred to, one that was quite unconnected with the more renowned Dublin bakery of the same name. A few years ago it had been suggested to him that he should consider retitling his, calling it Ideal Bread and Cakes, or Ovenfresh, in order to avoid confusion, but he saw no need for that, believing, indeed, that if a change should come about it should be made by the Dublin firm.

'I want to thank you,' Lairdman said, 'for taking all this so well. Annabella has told me.'

'I doubt I have an option.'

Lairdman's lips were notably thin, his mouth a narrow streak that smiled without apparent effort. He smiled a little now, but shook his head to dispel any misconception: he was not gloating, he was not agreeing that his mistress's husband had no option. Boland was surprised that he didn't have a little chopped-off moustache, as so many Dublin men had.

'I thought when we met you might hit me,' Lairdman said. 'I remarked that to Annabella, but she said that wasn't you at all.'

'No, it isn't me.'

'That's what I mean by taking it well.'

'All I want to know is what you have in mind. She doesn't seem to know herself.'

'In mind?'

'I'm not protesting at your intentions where my wife is concerned, only asking if you're thinking of marrying her, only asking if you have some kind of programme. I mean, have you a place up here that's suitable for her? You're not a married man, I understand? I'll have another J.J.,' Boland called out to the barman.

'No, I'm not a married man. What we were hoping was that—if you're agreeable—Annabella could move herself into my place more or less at once. It's suitable accommodation all right, a seven-room flat in Wellington Road. But in time we'll get a house.'

'Thanks,' Boland said to the barman, paying him more money.

'That was my turn,' Lairdman protested, just a little late.

She wouldn't care for meanness, Boland thought. She'd notice when it began to impinge on her, which in time it would: these things never mattered at first.

'But marriage?' he said. 'It isn't easy, you know, to marry another man's wife in Ireland.'

It's Platonic

This poem is by Rita Ann Higgins, from the collection
Philomena's Revenge.

Platonic my eye,

I yearn
for the fullness
of your tongue
making me
burst forth
pleasure after pleasure
after dark,

soaking all my dreams.

Epilogue

The Van

*This extract is from the final part of Roddy Doyle's 'Barrytown
Trilogy',* The Van, *published in 1991. The quotation was an
irresistible temptation to use as an epilogue: it sums up the
whole situation of romance, love and sex in Ireland.
On the other hand, perhaps it sums it down.*

That was the first time they'd done the business in a good
while; two months nearly. Made love. He'd never called it
that; it sounded thick. Riding your wife was more than just
riding, especially when yis hadn't done it in months, but—he could
never have said Let's make love to Veronica; she'd have burst out
laughing at him.

205

Acknowledgments

For permission to use copyright material, grateful acknowledgment is made to the following:

Penguin Books for extracts from *The Railway Station Man* by Jennifer Johnston, © Jennifer Johnston, Hamish Hamilton 1984 and *Out After Dark* by Hugh Leonard, © Hugh Leonard 1989, first published by Andre Deutsch;

Secker & Warburg, Publishers for an extract from *The Van* by Roddy Doyle, © Roddy Doyle;

Blackstaff Press for permission to reproduce 'Felicity in Turin' by Paul Durcan and 'For Roberta in the Garden' by John Hewitt;

Poolbeg Group Services Ltd for permission to reproduce 'It's Platonic' by Rita Ann Higgins, 'Afterlove' by Moya Cannon and 'Flesh ... the Greatest Sin' by Eithne Strong;

Carcanet Press for permission to reproduce 'Exhibitionist' by Eavan Boland;

Harper Collins for an extract from *The Public World of Parable Jones* by Dominic Behan;

Only Women Press for 'White Light' by Mary Dorcey;

Oxford University Press for 'When the Ecstatic Body Grips' by Eric Dodds and the translation of 'The Lament of Créidhe, Daughter of Guaire of Aidhne' by Gerard Murphy, reprinted from *Early Irish Lyrics* edited and translated by Gerard Murphy (1956);

Constable & Company for an extract from the short story 'The Faithless Wife' from the collection *Foreign Affairs and Other Stories* by Seán O Faoláin;

Faber and Faber for 'Double Negative' and 'Displaced Person' by Richard Murphy, 'Poem for Marie', 'Act of Union' and 'Valediction' by Seamus Heaney, extracts from 'Autumn Journal' and 'Trilogy for X' by Louis MacNeice, 'I Would Like My Love to Die' by Samuel Beckett and an extract from *The Pornographer* by John McGahern;

A. P. Watt Ltd on behalf of Dermot Bolger for an extract from *Night Shift* by Dermot Bolger;

Peters, Fraser and Dunlop and the Estate of the late Frank O'Connor for the translation of 'The Midnight Court' and 'The Lament for Art O'Leary' by Frank O'Connor;

Mr Michael Longley for his 'Love Poems';

Gallery Press for 'On Not Being Your Lover' by Medbh McGuckian, 'Mo Mhíle Stór', 'Oileán' and 'I Cannot Lie Here' by Nuala Ní Dhomhnaill and 'The Net' by W. R. Rogers;

The Estate of the late Patrick Kavanagh for 'Bluebells for Love' by Patrick Kavanagh;

Neasa Ní Shé and the Irish Texts Society for the translation of 'The Pursuit of Diarmaid and Gráinne';

The Dedalus Press and Seán Mac Mathgamhna for translations of Úna Bhán, 'Dónall Óg' and 'Nóra Ní Chonchúir Bháin';

Wolfhound Press for an extract from *Goodbye to the Hill* by Lee Dunne.

Despite their best efforts, the Publishers were unable to trace the other copyright holders. They will, however, make the usual and appropriate arrangements with any who contact them.

Index of Authors

Index of Translators

A Dublin Anthology
Douglas Bennett

A Dublin Anthology is a panorama of writing by and about Dubliners and Dublin. It is divided into five main sections: fiction; social and cultural life; biography; history; and travel. All the great names are here: Beckett, Behan, Joyce, Yeats and all the other giants. There are also some surprises. Winston Churchill spent part of his youth in Dublin when his father was Lord Lieutenant of Ireland and the book includes an extract from *My Early Life*. Chiang Yee sees the city through the eyes of a late nineteenth/early twentieth century Chinese.

A Dublin Anthology reproduces extracts from newspapers, the memoirs of nuns, the journals of travellers, the reports of social enquirers, the histories of commercial concerns and the nostalgic recollections of Dubliners of many eras. The voices in this book are as varied as those of politicians, painters, policemen and prostitutes. Here you will find literary and social life cheek by jowl with the street life of the poor; in short, all the variegated experiences of a great city through the centuries.

£9.99 Paperback